THE BURDEN OF SØREN KIERKEGAARD

The Edward Carnell Library

An Introduction to Christian Apologetics,* 1948

Television: Servant or Master, 1950

The Theology of Reinhold Niebuhr, 1951

A Philosophy of the Christian Religion, 1952

A Christian Commitment,* 1957

The Case for Orthodox Theology,* 1959

The Kingdom of Love and the Pride of Life, 1960

The Burden of Søren Kierkegaard, 1965

The Case for Biblical Christianity,* 1969

*These reprint editions also include Edward Carnell's Presidential Inaugural Address, "The Glory of a Theological Seminary," presented at Fuller Seminary in 1955. This appears at the end of these books.

The Burden of Søren Kierkegaard

by

EDWARD JOHN CARNELL

PROFESSOR OF ETHICS AND PHILOSOPHY OF RELIGION
FULLER THEOLOGICAL SEMINARY

WIPF & STOCK · Eugene, Oregon

Wipf and Stock Publishers
199 W 8th Ave, Suite 3
Eugene, OR 97401

The Burden of Soren Kierkegaard
By Carnell, Edward J.
Copyright©1965 Becker, Jean Carnell and Carnell, John
ISBN 13: 978-1-55635-147-1
ISBN 10: 1-55635-147-X
Publication date 12/15/2006
Previously published by Wm. B. Eerdmans, 1965

Affectionately dedicated to Dr. Phillip H. Wells, chief psychiatrist of the Wells Medical Group, Arcadia, California; without whose personal encouragement it is unlikely that I would have attempted to write this book.

Foreword

Edward J. Carnell (1919–1967) is one of the most fascinating figures in twentieth-century American evangelicalism. By age forty he had produced a corpus of major writings more impressive than many scholars produce in a far longer lifetime. Nor was he, like some, writing essentially the same book in differing forms. His writing was marked both by creativity and by remarkable development during his relatively short productive career. He was also, by all accounts, the most popular teacher at Fuller Theological Seminary, where he taught from 1948 until 1967 and served as president from 1954 to 1959. For a few years, at the peak of his brief career, he was regarded as the leading intellectual representative of evangelicalism in the larger American theological community. Although his writings are today not as well-known as they were in the past—a regrettable situation that we can hope this volume will begin to remedy—he played a major role in setting the tone for much of future evangelicalism, especially the kind of approach represented these days at Fuller Theological Seminary.

The son of a Baptist pastor, Carnell received his BA from Wheaton College, where he was influenced by the philosopher Gordon H. Clark (1902–1986). Graduating from Wheaton in 1941, Carnell went on to Westminster Theological Seminary where he studied with apologist Cornelius Van Til (1895–1987). In 1944, the same year that Carnell completed his BD at Westminster, Clark and Van Til became engaged in a sharp controversy concerning Clark's more rationalistic apologetic and Van Til's presuppositional approach. Carnell, who sided with Clark, was searching for his own resolution of these differences. He also sought to engage the Protestant intellectual mainstream of the day, going on to Harvard Divinity School for a ThD, where he wrote on Reinhold Niebuhr. While in the Boston area he enrolled in a second doctoral program in philosophy at Boston University. He wrote his doctoral dissertation there on Søren Kierkegaard and received his PhD in 1949. Eventually he turned these works into books on these prominent figures.

More remarkably, while he was engaged in these two doctoral programs, he produced his first major book, *An Introduction to Christian Apologetics*, published in 1948. This volume, which addressed issues that Carnell had been wrestling with in his studies with Clark and Van Til, received the "Evangelical Book Award" of $5,000 (a comfortable year's salary) from William B. Eerdmans Publishing Company.

When in 1948 Carnell took a position at Fuller Theological Seminary in Pasadena, California, he was already established as a prodigy of the "new evangelical" movement that was emerging out of fundamentalism. Fuller Seminary had been founded just the previous year to be the intellectual flagship of this movement. Harold J. Ockenga (1905–1985), pastor of Park Street Church in Boston, was the leader of this movement and served as Fuller Seminary's president *in absentia*. Fundamentalist radio evangelist Charles E. Fuller (1887–1968) provided solid funding. The seminary was to be made up of theological "stars" of the movement and Carnell joined Carl F. H. Henry (1913–2003) as one of the brightest younger lights.

Having accomplished so much before the age of thirty, Carnell had the highest ambitions for the movement of which he was a part and for his role in it. In his efforts to revolutionize evangelical apologetics, he frankly aspired to be the evangelical equivalent of Paul Tillich or Reinhold Niebuhr, the best-known Protestant theologians of the era; he looked to have, as these theologians did, a major national audience. His hopes to be a popular commentator soon met with disillusion when his small book, *Television: Servant or Master?* (1950), despite its balanced approach, proved to be a commercial failure. Nonetheless, his determination to change the face of the theological world remained intact.

In 1952 he published a second major work on apologetics, *A Philosophy of the Christian Religion*. In this he departed from his earlier emphasis on the law of non-contradiction and "systematic consistency" and emphasized more that Christianity best satisfied the heart's desire for meaningful values. Five years later, in 1957, he published a third apologetic work, *Christian Commitment: An Apologetic*, this time with a major commercial publisher, Macmillan in New York. Addressing Christianity's "cultured despisers," this highly original volume emphasized the existential appeal of Christianity. Particularly Carnell emphasized the commonalities between the experiences of believers and non-believers and how Christianity best accounts for universal moral sentiments, such as moral outrage or a sense of injustice. The book, although creative, did not have the impact that Carnell hoped. Part of the problem was that Carnell, despite his immense intelligence, was less and less working within a tradition. Béla Vassady, a distinguished Reformed theologian from Hungary who was briefly a colleague of Carnell, later commented that he was amazed at the degree Carnell believed he could reconstruct Christian thought on his own. Theologian John G. Stackhouse Jr. has suggested that Carnell was a sort of "intellectual Thoreau," depending on insights into his own experience and then generalizing to all humanity. These perceived traits may help to explain why Carnell did not gain a larger public constituency.

In the meantime Carnell had been elevated to the presidency of Fuller Theological Seminary where he encountered some other problems. In May 1955 he delivered his inaugural address, "The Glory of a Theological Seminary." In it he emphasized the need for mutual tolerance and for emphasizing Christian love over fine points of theological difference. Fuller Seminary in 1955 was too close to its partly fundamentalist origins for these sentiments to pass unchallenged. Conservatives on the faculty suggested that Carnell's sentiments smacked of theological compromise and blocked the publication of his address. (Only after Carnell's death did his former student, President David Hubbard of Fuller Seminary, have it published.)

The controversy over Carnell's inaugural address at Fuller was part of the background for the most controversial part of his much-discussed book, *The Case for Orthodox Theology* (1959). By the later

1950s, even though Carnell had not had the national impact for which he had hoped, he did have the satisfaction that mainline Protestant leaders were recognizing him as one of the most thoughtful evangelical spokesmen. He was honored to play this role when he was chosen by Westminster Press to write a book on evangelicalism to complement books on Protestant liberalism and neo-orthodoxy in a three-part series. While Carnell defended broadly Reformed orthodoxy, the most notable part of his book was his polemic against fundamentalism. Not only did he attack dispensationalist theology and fundamentalist anti-intellectualism, but he also singled out conservative Protestantism's most renowned scholar, J. Gresham Machen (1881–1937), for some of his strongest criticism. Carnell characterized Machen, the founder of Westminster Theological Seminary and the Orthodox Presbyterian Church, as promoting a "cultic mentality" which Carnell saw as one of the worst features of fundamentalism. Even though Carnell had resigned from the Fuller presidency at just about the same time that *The Case for Orthodoxy* appeared, the book brought widespread criticism from conservatives and fundamentalists to Fuller Theological Seminary and to its sponsor, Charles E. Fuller.

Carnell resigned the presidency largely because of deteriorating mental health. His condition was doubtless exacerbated by the immense pressures of the presidency while also continuing with his scholarship. In the subsequent years he suffered from bouts of severe depression and during the worst period in 1961–62 he was hospitalized for five weeks and then continued an extensive series of shock treatments or electroconvulsive therapy. Nonetheless, he continued his teaching and some writing, although as a teacher he was only a shadow of himself. He also maintained his role as an evangelical spokesperson on the national scene, continuing to write for the *Christian Century* and other journals articles that would be collected posthumously in *The Case for Biblical Christianity*, edited by Ronald H. Nash. Most notably he accepted, despite his illness, the great honor of being one of the "young theologians" chosen to dialogue with theologian Karl Barth on his much-heralded visit to the United States in 1962.

Before the most severe onset of his illness, Carnell had completed yet another apologetic work, *The Kingdom of Love and the Pride of Life* (1960). Once again he shifted his emphasis and tone. In dealing with his psychological difficulties he had been reading Freud and he incorporated insights from modern psychology into his work. As in much of his writing, he generalized from personal insight into the human condition. In this case he emphasized the universal need for love that Christianity offered as a counter to destructive pride. His only major publication after his illness was *The Burden of Søren Kierkegaard*, which drew on work he had done for his Boston University doctoral dissertation.

In May of 1967 Carnell was to be one of three keynote speakers at a Roman Catholic ecumenical conference in Oakland, California. On the day of the conference he was found dead in his hotel room from an apparent accidental overdose of sleeping pills.

Carnell's spectacular successes, his even higher ambitions, his disappointments, and his profound inner struggles make him one of the most intriguing figures in this history of American evangelicalism. His writings often combine incisive logic with introspection. In them one can both find the products of one of the finest minds of the time and get glimpses of what might be characterized as "the burden of Edward J. Carnell."

—George M. Marsden
2007

PREFACE

After reflecting on the system of Kierkegaard for a reasonable span of time, I have finally rallied courage to express myself on a portion of this system. I sincerely hope that what I say is marked by accuracy.

Apart from a few critical remarks — in footnotes and in the text — and apart from half of what is at most a brief terminal chapter, my approach to Kierkegaard is affirmative rather than negative. I have inserted a generous number of quotations from Kierkegaard's own books, in order that the reader might have an opportunity to evaluate the primary material for himself.

Since there are so many possible approaches to the system of Kierkegaard, I have deliberately confined myself to what I feel are two central theses, namely, "existential living" and the baffling thesis which meant so much to Kierkegaard, "Truth is subjectivity." Naturally I wandered away at times, but not excessively — at least this is my opinion.

I cheerfully acknowledge an indebtedness to the following publishers for the specific editions of Kierkegaard's works (plus a few secondary sources) which I used in the writing of this volume: To the Augsburg Publishing House for Kierkegaard, *The Gospel of Suffering*, 1948, translated by David F. Swenson and Lillian Marvin Swenson; and David F. Swenson, *Something About Kierkegaard*, 1948. To the William B. Eerdmans Publishing Company for Kierkegaard, *The Gospel of Our Sufferings*, 1964, translated by A. S. Aldworth and W. S. Ferrie. To Lutterworth Press, London and Redhill, for Denzil G. M. Patrick, *Pas-*

cal and Kierkegaard, A Study in the Strategy of Evangelism, 1947. To Harper & Brothers for Kierkegaard, *Purity of Heart Is To Will One Thing,* 1938, translated with an Introductory Essay by Douglas V. Steere. To Harper Torchbooks for Kierkegaard, *The Point of View For My Work as an Author,* 1962, translated with Introduction and Notes by Walter Lowrie — newly edited with a preface by Benjamin Nelson. To Oxford University Press for Kierkegaard's *Christian Discourses* and *The Lilies of the Field and the Birds of the Air* and *Three Discourses at the Communion on Fridays,* 1961, translated with an Introduction by Walter Lowrie; for *The Journals of Sören Kierkegaard,* 1951, a selection edited and translated by Alexander Dru; for Walter Lowrie, *Kierkegaard,* 1938; for Kierkegaard's *The Present Age* and *Two Minor Ethico-Religious Treatises,* 1949, translated by Alexander Dru and Walter Lowrie, with an Introduction by Charles Williams; for Theodor Haecker, *Sören Kierkegaard,* 1937, translated and with a biographical note by Alexander Dru. To Princeton University Press, for Kierkegaard, *Attack Upon "Christendom,"* 1944, translated, with an Introduction, by Walter Lowrie; for Kierkegaard's *The Concept of Dread,* 1946, translated, with Introduction and Notes, by Walter Lowrie; for Kierkegaard's *Concluding Unscientific Postscript,* 1944, translated by David F. Swenson, and completed after his death and provided with Introduction and Notes by Walter Lowrie; for Kierkegaard, *Either/Or,* 1946, volume one translated by David F. Swenson and Lillian Marvin Swenson, volume two translated by Walter Lowrie; for Kierkegaard, *Fear and Trembling,* 1945, translated, with Introduction and Notes, by Walter Lowrie; for Kierkegaard, *For Self-Examination and Judge For Yourselves!* and *Three Discourses,* 1944, translated by Walter Lowrie; for Robert Bretall, *A Kierkegaard Anthology,* 1947; for Kierkegaard, *Philosophical Fragments,* 1946, translated, with Introduction and Notes, by David F. Swenson; for Kierkegaard, *Repetition,* 1946, translated, with Introduction and Notes, by Walter Lowrie; for Walter Lowrie, *A Short Life of Kierkegaard,* 1946; for Kierkegaard, *The Sickness Unto Death,* 1946, translated, with an Introduction, by Walter Lowrie; for Kierkegaard, *Stages On Life's Way,* 1945, translated by Walter Lowrie; for Kierkegaard,

Training in Christianity and the Edifying Discourse, 1947, translated, with an Introduction and Notes, by Walter Lowrie; for Kierkegaard, *Works of Love,* 1946, translated by David F. Swenson and Lillian Marvin Swenson, with an Introduction by Douglas V. Steere. To Charles Scribner's Sons for Reinhold Niebuhr, *The Nature and Destiny of Man,* 1946. To the Wisdom Library, a division of Philosophical Library, for Kierkegaard, *The Diary,* 1960, translated by Gerda M. Andersen, edited by Peter P. Rohde.

—EDWARD JOHN CARNELL

CONTENTS

Preface		7
ONE:	The Foundation of Kierkegaard's Burden	13
TWO:	Kierkegaard's Vocation	26
THREE:	Kierkegaard's View of Man	43
FOUR:	The Dialectic of Inwardness	56
FIVE:	Kingdom Outcasts	90
SIX:	Subjective Truth	124
SEVEN:	Yes and No	165
Index		173

Chapter One

THE FOUNDATION OF KIERKEGAARD'S BURDEN

A. *By Way of Introduction*

EVERY HUMAN BEING REFLECTS THE UNIQUENESS BROUGHT ON by the combined influences of heredity, environment, personal health, experience, education, and native intellectual, spiritual, and psychological gifts. Only an Aristotle could have conceived the vast potency-act system of philosophy, and only an Aquinas could have devised such erudite means by which to blend the presuppositions of Aristotle with those of Christianity. Only a Spinoza could have contrived an ethic *sub quandam aeternitatis*, and only a Kant could have created such a rationally technical series of *Critiques*.

In the event that a human being is a genius — as was each philosopher cited in the paragraph above, and as was Kierkegaard himself — the most commonplace insight can be developed to the point where it impresses others as something unique, if not world shaking.

There is little doubt that Sören Kierkegaard (1813-1855) was a genius, for he wrote a small library of stimulating books. Many of these books have been translated into all the major languages of the world.

But Kierkegaard was a genius plagued by personal idiosyncrasies. Denzil G. M. Patrick observes the following:

> Kierkegaard was a neurotic: of that the story of his life leaves little doubt. His heritage, physique, temperament, upbringing and way of life were all abnormal, and produced a perpetual maladjustment between him and his environment. His *Journals* are a happy hunting-ground for the psycho-analyst.[1]

But neither Patrick nor others imply that Kierkegaard's idiosyncrasies disqualified him from engaging in the pursuit of truth. On the contrary, a number of great writers have asserted that neurotic pressures inside an individual create a painful feeling of maladjustment to life; and that this feeling, in turn, may prompt the suffering individual to take up the pen and tell what he believes is man's relation to reality, as well as to spell out the responsibilities which accompany that relation. In other words, the slightest spiritual, rational, or emotional impression on the psyche may be used as a clue to the meaning of life in general.

Walter Lowrie effectively warns that it is hazardous to try to draw an easy line between those who are normal and those who are not.

> It will not do to dispose of S. K.'s psychology by remarking that his own soul, the soul he chiefly studied, was a sick soul. For not only could he reply that all souls are sick, and that the notion that one has a "healthy-minded" soul is the most perilous of all sicknesses; but all pathologists will agree with him that the study of abnormal states is essential for the understanding of normal health. If it is true that few men have had so sick a soul to deal with as had S. K., and also that no one of them has ever probed so deeply into his sick soul, with such intellectual competence, we may reasonably expect to learn something from his psychology.[2]

The passage of time has only served to confirm the wisdom of Lowrie's observation; for students of psychology, as well as students of theology and philosophy of religion, continue to

---

[1] Patrick, *Pascal and Kierkegaard*, II, 311. Lutterworth Press, London and Redhill, 1947.
[2] Kierkegaard, *The Concept of Dread*, p. xii. Princeton University Press, Princeton, 1946. Translated by Walter Lowrie.

pore over Kierkegaard's works with something approaching a sense of reverence.

B. *Early Influences*

Kierkegaard's genius tended to rob him of those carefree hours in which a young boy paddles a raft down a river or goes in search of treasure on the side of some distant hill. He seemed to leap from infancy to manhood without passing through the happy stage of childhood.

> I never knew the joy of being a child. The terrible agonies I suffered disturbed the calm which is the constituent of childhood, of having it in one's power to be industrious, to please one's father; for the unrest within me resulted in my always, always being outside myself.[3]

Again — only this time we must approach Kierkegaard through the pseudonym, H. H.:

> .... as a child he was already an old man ... and so he lived on, he never grew any *younger*. An almost insane reversal of nature, a child who never grew young, a child who was already an old man and never grew younger. Oh, a terrible expression for a terrible suffering.[4]

All of this helps confirm the paradox that Kierkegaard's limitations helped serve as a useful taskmaster. He suffered "a certain bashfulness,"[5] for he was ever conscious of his personal limitations. Being "slight, delicate, and weak, denied in almost every respect the physical requirements necessary in order to be able to pass for a complete man as compared with others,"[6] he was haunted by a feeling of inferiority to the very end of his life.

> In addition to the wide circle of my acquaintances with whom I am, on the whole, on a very formal footing, I still have an intimate, confidential friend — my melancholy, and in the midst

---

[3] *The Journals of Sören Kierkegaard*, 860. Translated and edited by Alexander Dru, Oxford University Press, London, 1938. I have chosen to use this edition, rather than that which has recently appeared in the Harper Torchbooks, because it is more comprehensive in its selection of the material, and because its system of references is so handy.
[4] *Ibid.*, 921.
[5] *Ibid.*, 875.
[6] *Ibid.*, 1335.

of my pleasure, in the midst of my work, she beckons to me, calls me aside, even though physically I remain where I am, she is the most faithful mistress I have known, what wonder then that I must be ready to follow her at any moment of the day.[7]

Nonetheless, Kierkegaard realized that he was not altogether helpless, of course. ". . . melancholy, soul-sick, profoundly and absolutely a failure in many ways, one thing was given to me: a pre-eminent intelligence, presumably so that I should not be quite defenceless."[8] Thus, his intelligence worked *with,* as well as *against,* the feeling of melancholy.

> While I am submerged in the deepest suffering of melancholy, some thought or other becomes so knotted up that I cannot disentangle it, and since it is connected with my own life I suffer incredibly. And then after a certain time has gone by, the abscess bursts — and underneath lies the richest and most beautiful material for work and of the very kind I need at that moment.[9]

Kierkegaard, in speaking about the "crazy way" in which he had been brought up, anticipated one of the major presuppositions of modern psychotherapy: *i.e.,* that many factors in mental illness can be traced to traumatic experiences suffered in childhood.

> The thoughtlessness, carelessness, and cocksureness with which children are brought up is frightful to see and yet everyone is essentially what they are to be when they are ten years old; and yet one would find that almost everyone bears with them a defect from their childhood, which they do not overcome even in their seventieth year; together with the fact that all unhappy individuals are related to a false impression received in childhood. Oh, piteous satire upon mankind; that providence should have endowed almost every child so richly because it knew in advance what was to befall it: to be brought up by 'parents' *i.e.* to be made a mess of in every possible way.[10]

Not the least of the adverse home influences was that which grew out of the zeal to see that Kierkegaard persevered in the orthodox traditions of Christianity. "Humanly speaking my

[7] *Ibid.,* 359.
[8] *Ibid.,* 1335.
[9] *Ibid.,* 807.
[10] *Ibid.,* 927.

misfortune has clearly been that I was given a strict Christian upbringing — and that I have to live in so-called Christendom."[11]

But once again, quite happily, the misfortune of the home converted to a means which helped the anxious genius to gain a base from which to develop his conception of man's relation to reality. "The sternness of the parental discipline, indeed, gave the boy a lofty impression of duty, for he was trained to a strict obedience. . . . This left a permanent mark upon his thought."[12]

Kierkegaard's father, Michael Pedersen, exerted a lifelong influence over his brilliant, eccentric son. "I owe everything, from the beginning, to my father. When melancholy as he was, he saw me melancholy, his prayer to me was: Be sure that you really love Jesus Christ."[13] The father was not only religiously severe, but he suffered a great deal of personal anxiety when several of his children, along with his wife, died. Being an individual from whom "melancholy descended in inheritance,"[14] Michael Pedersen created within his son a sort of dialectical response of sympathy-antipathy, a response not unlike that which Kierkegaard later developed under the somewhat cryptic concept of *dread*. Thus, the fears suffered in the home contributed their part to the development of Kierkegaard's distorted understanding of divine love and grace.

> It is terrible when I think, even for a single moment, over the dark background which, from the very earliest time, was part of my life. The dread with which my father filled my soul, his own frightful melancholy, and all the things in this connection which I do not even note down. I felt a dread of Christianity and yet felt myself so strongly drawn towards it.[15]

We can appreciate the role played by anxiety when we recall the incident which prompted Kierkegaard to entertain the fear that he had to share in the guilt which his father incurred for

---

[11] *Ibid.*, 892.
[12] David F. Swenson, *Something About Kierkegaard*, p. 73. Augsburg Publishing House, Minneapolis, 1941.
[13] Kierkegaard, *Journals*, 773.
[14] *Ibid.*, 600.
[15] *Ibid.*, 841.

ostensibly blaspheming the name of God. "How terrible about the man who once as a little boy, while herding the flocks on the heaths of Jutland, suffering greatly, in hunger and in want, stood upon a hill and cursed God — and the man was unable to forget it even when he was eighty-two years old."[16] Let us remember that the father *was* eighty-two years old when he died. Thus, Kierkegaard's intellect, memory, and imagination instantly combined to form a shattering conspiracy.

> Then it was that the great earthquake occurred, the terrible revolution which suddenly forced upon me a new and infallible law of interpretation of all the facts. Then I suspected that my father's great age was not a divine blessing but rather a curse; that the outstanding intellectual gifts of our family were only given to us in order that we should rend each other to pieces: then I felt the stillness of death grow around me when I saw in my father, an unhappy man who was to outlive us all, a cross on the tomb of all his hopes. There must be a guilt upon the whole family, the punishment of God must be on it; it was to disappear, wiped out by the powerful hand of God, obliterated like an unsuccessful attempt, and only at times did I find a little alleviation in the thought that my father had been allotted the heavy task of calming us with the consolation of religion, of ministering to us so that a better world should be open to us even though we lost everything in this world, even though we were overtaken by the punishment which the Jews always called down upon their enemies: that all recollection of us should be utterly wiped out, that we should no longer be found.[17]

As Kierkegaard appraised things, therefore, "a son is like a mirror in which the father beholds himself, and for the son the father too is like a mirror in which he beholds himself in the time to come."[18]

Although Kierkegaard made many references to his father, one searches in vain for any references to his mother. Some biographers suggest that she was not a mother in the best sense of the term, and thus she exerted very little moral influence on her son. In any case, Kierkegaard's failure to understand his

---

[16] *Ibid.*, 556.
[17] *Ibid.*, 243.
[18] Kierkegaard, *Stages on Life's Way*, p. 192. Princeton University Press, Princeton, 1945. Translated by Walter Lowrie.

mother may have contributed a great deal to his distorted view of both women and marriage in general.

> The fact that there was something which impeded S. K. from honoring his mother and from loving her as a son ought, was certainly a principal cause of his tragedy, and perhaps it accounts in part for the particular misfortune that he was not able to 'realize the universal' by marrying the woman he loved. He who wrote so much about woman, and so beautifully, though at the end so spitefully, was able to think of her only as the counterpart of man, and except when he wrote about 'Mary the Mother of God' he rarely dwelt upon the noblest and tenderest aspect of woman as mother.[19]

On the other hand, the fact that Kierkegaard "was always humorous, often whimsical . . ."[20] probably can be credited to his mother's influence, for such traits never came from his father. If this inference is correct, then criticism must cease, for one of the most unique elements in Kierkegaard's writing is his use of cutting irony and disarming humor.

It would take a most conceited student of past events to set out to define the exact manner in which Kierkegaard was *victimized* by his early life, and the exact manner in which he was *not*. Certainly he was a victim to some degree, as we all are. But the main point, Feuerbach notwithstanding,[21] is that Kierkegaard remarkably triumphed over the limitations which he faced because of his early life. He not only was convinced that the existing individual possesses a creative will, but he

---

[19] Walter Lowrie, *A Short Life of Kierkegaard*, p. 25. Princeton University Press, Princeton, 1946. A sample of Kierkegaard's prejudice: "Friendship is dangerous, marriage still more so; for woman is and ever will be the ruin of a man, as soon as he contracts a permanent relation with her. Take a young man who is fiery as an Arabian courser, let him marry, he is lost. Woman is first proud, then is she weak, then she swoons, then he swoons, then the whole family swoons. A woman's love is nothing but dissimulation and weakness." Kierkegaard, *Either/Or*, I, 244. Princeton University Press, Princeton, 1946. Translated by David F. Swenson and Lillian Marvin Swenson.

[20] Walter Lowrie, *Kierkegaard*, p. 60. Oxford University Press, London, 1938.

[21] There is something self-destructive about Feuerbach's materialistic premise that man is what he eats; for then even the thesis itself — that man is what he eats — is a result of what *Feuerbach* ate, and thus it is stripped of all universal reference.

himself personally expressed this power of creation over and over again in his writings. In fact, it was his dream to soar into the world of spirit, where the only limit to being was the self-satisfied state of the individual himself.

Lowrie very convincingly describes the kind of balanced judgment that a person should have when setting the victimized Kierkegaard next to the free Kierkegaard.

> At this point I ought perhaps to say that no one is less inclined than I to believe that the character of Kierkegaard was fixed, his fate determined and his life explained by inheritance and environment. These factors, of course, exerted a prodigious influence, which to a certain extent we can trace; S. K. attained an understanding of himself by reviewing his life from early childhood, and he had an unusually vivid feeling of solidarity with "the family, the clan, the race"; but on the other hand, the freedom and responsibility of the individual was his most ardent conviction, and therefore he accounted "the individual higher than the race." I know that I should encounter his scathing disapproval if in the manner of materialistic historians I were to endeavor to account for him by this background of inheritance and environment.[22]

C. *Later Life*

Kierkegaard bore a physical limitation which traced — as he supposed — to a fall from a tree in childhood. (See in this connection, Theodor Haecker, *Kierkegaard The Cripple*. Philosophical Library, New York, 1950. Translated by C. Van O. Bruyn.) The open taunts from others were not easy to bear, of course. But it can be safely said that Kierkegaard's suffering from a curvature of the spine helped him to despair of temporal fulfillment and to live for eternity. Being spared the conceit and pride which physical attractiveness generally spawns, Kierkegaard found himself in a far more natural condition to proceed with the task of detailing the topography of spirit.

But each time Kierkegaard supposed that he was free to leave Christianity, he was confronted with a new catalogue of fears. These fears, in turn, helped him in his understanding of the "dread of spirit," an understanding which was given such a

---

[22] Lowrie, *A Short Life of Kierkegaard*, pp. 29-30.

prominent place in his later writings. Dread is the "dizziness of freedom which occurs when the spirit would posit the synthesis, and freedom then gazes down into its own possibility, grasping at finiteness to sustain itself. In this dizziness freedom succumbs."[23] Again,

> The nature of original sin has often been examined, and yet the principal category has been missing — it is *dread,* that is what really determines it; for dread is a desire for what one fears, a sympathetic antipathy; dread is an alien power which takes hold of the individual, and yet one cannot extricate oneself from it, does not wish to, because one is afraid, but what one fears attracts one. Dread renders the individual powerless, and the first sin always happens in a moment of weakness; it therefore lacks any apparent accountableness, but that want is the real snare.[24]

In an effort to control this dizziness of freedom, Kierkegaard turned to a study of philosophy. "He studied it, therefore, in the only way that it can be profitably studied, that is, for his own consumption, with a view to discovering a meaning in his life, when meaning had vanished with the rejection of Christianity."[25] And since Hegel was all the rage at the time, it was only natural that Kierkegaard studied Hegel with great dedication and passion.

But the feeling of dread which accompanies individual freedom simply would not subside. Hence, the more Kierkegaard sought relief in Hegel, the more he suffered spiritual discontent — especially with Hegel's vain and overweening concept of "immanence." Immanence implies the metaphysical assumption that God and man share such a similar rational and moral environment that man is free to address God with no more fear and trembling than he would have if he were addressing a cowboy or a neighbor.[26]

Reference to Regina Olsen is necessary at this point. One can only wonder what Kierkegaard's burden would have been like if he had had the courage to marry Regina, and if their marriage had been crowned with mutual happiness. But such

---

[23] Kierkegaard, *The Concept of Dread,* p. 55.
[24] Kierkegaard, *Journals,* 402.
[25] Lowrie, *op. cit.,* p. 115.
[26] The question of immanence will be taken up again in a later chapter.

a wonder must remain in the territory of imagination, for the fact is that Kierkegaard did *not* have courage to marry Regina, and that as a result of this withdrawal he inflicted great damage on his psyche.

Curiously enough, however, the difficulty did not stem from a failure on Kierkegaard's part to play a successful role as lover, for he not only won the heart of the maiden but he was given permission to proceed with the rite of marriage. The main trouble, as one might suspect, stemmed from a new outcropping of dread. The more Kierkegaard reminded himself that he was taking on the life of another human being, the more he was gripped by an incapacitating fear. The marriage might fail. Then what? Deeming it the only proper thing to do, therefore, he broke his engagement with Regina. Such rash action did *not* deliver him from fear, of course, for now he was frightened by the thought of the hurt he had caused.

Nonetheless, Regina continued as the reigning queen in Kierkegaard's life, for the consuming love which he first felt never left him. He spoke of her as "thou sovereign of my heart, treasured in the deepest fastness of my breast, in the fullness of my thought. . . ."[27] Yet all the while fear continued to eat away like a cancer. ". . . I was frightened by the ideal; and so I gave birth to deformities, and therefore reality does not answer to my burning desires, — O God, grant that that should not also be the case in love; for there too I am seized by a mysterious dread of having confused an ideal with a reality. God forbid! Until now that is not the case. But that dread makes me long to know the future, and yet fear it! —"[28] This kind of introspection is echoed in many of Kierkegaard's writings — such as *Fear and Trembling, Repetition,* and *Stages on Life's Way.* Kierkegaard was deeply hurt by what he looked upon as a failure to complete the universal.

Nonetheless, the persistence of his affection for Regina goaded him on to become a more prolific writer. "Alas, she could not break the silence of my melancholy. That I loved her —

[27] Kierkegaard, *Journals,* 259.
[28] *Ibid.,* 333.

nothing is more certain — and thus my melancholy received enough to feed upon, oh, it received a terrible addition. It is essentially owing to her, to my melancholy and to my money that I became an author."[29]

Misunderstood and mocked in Copenhagen, the frustrated lover fled to Berlin for refuge. Here he began to write what, in effect, was a series of notes to Regina. His main purpose was to convince her that he was nothing but a plain wastrel. For example, much of the ponderous aesthetic work, *Either/Or*, was addressed to Regina. In the "Diary of the Seducer" he wrote the following:

> By the aid of his intellectual endowments he had known how to tempt a young girl and attract her to himself, without really caring to possess her. I can imagine that he knew how to excite a girl to the highest pitch, so that he was certain that she was ready to sacrifice everything. When the affair reached this point, he broke off without himself having made the slightest advances, and without having let fall a single word of love, let alone a declaration, a promise. And still it had happened, and the consciousness of it was doubly bitter for the unhappy girl because there was not the slightest thing to which she could appeal, because she was constantly tossed about by her varying moods in a terrible witches' dance, in which she alternately reproached herself and forgave him, then presently reproached him, and then, since the relationship had had reality only in a figurative sense, she must constantly struggle with the doubt as to whether the whole affair was not a figment of the imagination.[30]

Since Kierkegaard was continually plagued by the fear of dread, he never seriously entertained the hope of becoming reconciled with Regina. So when he returned to Copenhagen and suspected that Regina had not yet fully understood what a wretch of a man he was, he sat down and dashed off two highly poetical works in the space of only two months — *Repetition* and *Fear and Trembling*. Just as he was about to send the final draft of *Repetition* to the publisher, however,

---

[29] *Ibid.*, 748.
[30] Kierkegaard, *Either/Or*, I, 254. Princeton University Press, Princeton, 1946. Translated by David F. Swenson and Lillian Marvin Swenson.

Kierkegaard heard some information which didn't quite fit into the general picture which he had painted.

> At this point the strain of intense pathos was relieved by a touch of the comic. Just when the last chapter of *Repetition* had been concluded, and the hero had killed himself because he could not endure to think that his beloved was rendered desperate by his desertion — just at that moment S. K. learned that Regina was engaged to Fritz Schlegel. So the conclusion of the book had to be changed, the plan of it was marred, and its purpose was obscured.[31]

With almost sadistic delight Kierkegaard continued to conceal his authorship by a skillful use of pseudonyms, though all the while retaining the faint hope that Regina would grasp what he was driving at — despite his use of "indirect communication" as a primary literary device.

But even after Regina had pledged her life to Fritz Schlegel, thus releasing Kierkegaard to seal his engagement with God, he made a deliberate attempt to establish social fellowship with the Schlegels. When his attempt was openly rebuffed, however, he felt that he had no other course before him than to seek to establish his own individuality.

With incredible fecundity Kierkegaard continued to write volume after volume. Then in 1846, with the publication of the enormous philosophical-psychological-theological work, *Concluding Unscientific Postscript,* Kierkegaard decided that it was time to let up as an author.[32] "My idea is now to prepare myself for holy orders. I have prayed to God for several months to give me further help, for it has been clear to me for a long time past that I ought not to continue any longer as an author, which I either wish to be entirely and absolutely, or not at all."[33] But the momentum could not be terminated, for the spirit has a habit of continuing its wandering, once it has been aroused. *Works of Love, The Sickness Unto Death, Training in Christi-*

---

[31] Lowrie, *Kierkegaard,* p. 193.
[32] Lowrie very helpfully proposes that the word "unscientific" might better be rendered "simple."
[33] Kierkgaard, *Journals,* 555.

The Foundation of Kierkegaard's Burden 25

anity, The Point of View — all these, and other books, appeared subsequent to the *Concluding Unscientific Postscript*.[34]

Kierkegaard died on November 11, 1855. While he was furiously working on the last number of the *Instant*, still trying to translate his spiritual intuitions into words, Kierkegaard fell unconscious. Forty days later he died. Thus, God's faithful hound, heated from the chase, lay down to his eternal reward.

---

[34] Kierkegaard's complaint in the *Journals* has misled a number of readers. "And I hope my case will also be considered because other authors get small royalties from their books (though it may always be little enough), whereas I actually pay out money and my proof reader earns more than I do." 623. "Only recently (in 1935), Professor Brandt and Else Rommel carried out an investigation which exploded this myth and proved that he not only made a considerable profit on the books he published at his own expense, but that, beginning with August 1847, all his subsequent works, nine of them, besides the nine numbers of the *Instant*, were undertaken by the publishers, who paid him the usual royalties." Lowrie, *A Short Life of Kierkgaard*, p. 153.

Chapter Two

KIERKEGAARD'S VOCATION

A. *A Defense of the Individual*

Since Kierkegaard's manner of life offended those who thoughtlessly conformed to the dictates of the group, it was only natural that he would devote a generous portion of his writing to an upgrading of the individual and a downgrading of the group. Kierkegaard, as he marched off to war, thought he knew precisely where to pitch the battle, "for that is where the battle must be fought...."[1]

> How often have I shown that fundamentally Hegel makes men into heathens, *into a race of animals gifted with reason.* For in the animal world "the individual" is always less important than the race. But it is the peculiarity of the human race that just because the individual is created in the image of God "the individual" is above the race. This can be wrongly understood and terribly misused: *concedo.* But that is Christianity. And *that* is where the battle must be fought.[2]

Defending the individual was but another way of defending the spiritual responsibility of *freedom.*

> The most tremendous thing which has been granted to man is: the choice, freedom. And if you desire to save it and preserve it there is only one way: in the very same second uncon-

---

[1] Kierkgaard, *Journals,* 313.
[2] *Ibid.,* 1050.

ditionally and in complete resignation to give it back to God, and yourself with it. If the sight of what is granted to you tempts you, and if you give way to the temptation and look with egoistic desire upon the freedom of choice, then you lose your freedom. And your punishment is: to go on in a kind of confusion priding yourself on having — freedom of choice, but woe upon you, that is your judgment . . . .[3]

The tone of Kierkegaard's defense has something about it which is very relevant to our generation, for more and more, in our drift toward socialization and collectivism, we see evidences of the major tragedy that human beings are so afraid to become individuals that they cast their lot with the group. Through this expedient they hope to find meaning and dignity for their lives, but the exact opposite results, for the very qualities which sustain individuality are a threat to any universal expressions within the group.

The loss of individuality is not easily perceived, however, or if it is perceived, the magnitude of the tragedy is seldom appreciated. Conformists are so determined to be approved by the masses that they surrender the delicacy and sanctity of their God-given right to free expression. People from all walks of life, whether young or old, are terrified by the prospect of having to stand alone. And when enough people are willing to renounce their freedom, the way is paved for the introduction of either a top-heavy government or an outright dictatorship.

Before we proceed to canonize Kierkegaard, however, let us remember that self-interest played a very critical role in his motivation. By defending the duty of a person to be a free individual, and especially by blending this duty with that of being a Christian, Kierkegaard was actually engaged in a subtle defense of himself. As he saw the situation, any fool could throw away the dignity of his life by taking shelter in the group; but it took a man of both wisdom and courage to be a free, responsible self, come what may. Kierkegaard did not come right out and say so, of course, but he dropped modest hints here and there that he thought of himself as a rather accomplished person. Though being far from perfection, "yet had I to crave an in-

[3] *Ibid.*, 1051.

scription on my grave I would ask for none other than 'the individual'. . . ."⁴

Thus, the apology for the dignity of the individual was, in any event, a vocation which supplied Kierkegaard with a convenient means by which to establish his own individuality. At the same time it gave every outward appearance that he was exclusively concerned with the task of arousing both the city of Copenhagen and the Lutheran church. Be a Christian and an individual! This was his prophetic cry.

> Central in the thought of Sören Kierkegaard is his master category *the individual*. All of his thought ultimately had to pass through the needle's eye of whether or not it compelled men to face their sovereign responsibility as individuals. And this, too, was the pass of Thermopylae at which Kierkegaard stationed himself to defend the individual against any philosophical, political, or religious teaching that tended to slack off this consciousness of the individual's essential responsibility and integrity.⁵

It was only natural that Kierkegaard, when pursuing his work in philosophy, leaped for joy when he reviewed the vocation of Socrates. The Delphic epigram, "Know thyself!", was a reminder that temperance in all things, a state brought on by individual freedom and resolution, was to be sought with all one's might. What a man does inwardly is infinitely more important than what he does outwardly.⁶ Socrates strove to be a midwife. He so expressed himself that he sought to teach only what could actually be reduplicated in his own life. He was an enemy of those philosophies which encourage persons to take refuge behind speculative systems.

> It was thus Socrates understood himself, and thus he thought that everyone must understand himself, in the light of this understanding interpreting his relationship to each individual, with equal humility and with equal pride. He had the courage and self-possession to be sufficient unto himself, but also in his re-

⁴ *Ibid.*, 723.
⁵ Kierkegaard, *Purity of Heart Is to Will One Thing*, p. xiv. Harper & Brothers, New York and London, 1938. Translated by Douglas V. Steere.
⁶ Curiously enough, the fact that Socrates energetically sought connotative definitions, thus somewhat intellectualizing the maieutic science, did not seem to bother Kierkegaard.

lations to his fellowmen to be merely an occasion, even when dealing with the meanest capacity. How rare is such magnanimity![7]

There is no doubt that Kierkegaard drew consolation from the skilled manner in which Socrates claimed to be the wisest man in the world, solely on the ground that he *knew* that he didn't know; whereas others thought they knew, but in fact didn't know. Here was a perfect analogy, and Kierkegaard was not shy to draw on it. He didn't thrust himself forward as the most successful example of what it means to be an individual and a Christian, but he made it clear that those whom he addressed were farther from the ideal than he was.

Kierkegaard was equally excited by Socrates' use of the maieutic art, the method of dialogue and indirect communication which gave no one a right to claim possession of knowledge until he felt a personal responsibility for that claim. Socrates knew the game of the Sophists — how they strutted around as wise men, when all the while they made no effort to mediate their claims through passionate inwardness. Thus, Socrates was determined not to give answers plainly and openly, but rather, by maieutics, to bring his hearers to the place where they associated claims to knowledge with personal responsibility. Socrates, at best, was one who assisted others to give birth, but who himself gave no birth. He was firmly convinced — as was Kierkegaard — that he would cheat others if he did not force them to experience a stinging experience of their own ignorance. He realized that as long as ignorance is acknowledged, the possibility of future learning is kept open. But when a person smugly thinks that he knows, he cuts off this possibility.

Perhaps the most perfect illustration of the maieutic method is found in Plato's dialogue, *Euthyphro*. Here is a charming account of how Socrates conducted himself when he conversed with a young man (Euthyphro) who was on the way to prosecute his father for murder. Since Euthyphro seemed so sure of himself, Socrates set out at once to discover what the essence

---

[7] Kierkegaard, *Philosophical Fragments*, p. 7. Princeton University Press, Princeton, 1946. Translated by David F. Swenson.

of virtue was. "By the powers, Euthyphro! how little does the common herd know of the nature of right and truth. A man must be an extraordinary man, and have great strides in wisdom, before he could have seen his way to bring such an action."[8] As Euthyphro continued to give the impression that a knowledge of virtue was easy to obtain, Socrates declared: "Rare friend! I think that I cannot do better than be your disciple."[9] When Euthyphro took refuge behind illustrations of virtue — especially that which was illustrated by his own determination to prosecute his father for murder — Socrates reminded him that he was seeking connotative definitions, not illustrations. "Remember that I did not ask you to give me two or three examples of piety, but to explain the general idea which makes all pious things to be pious. Do you not recollect that there was one idea which made the impious impious, and the pious pious?"[10] Again, "Tell me what is the nature of this idea, and then I shall have a standard to which I may look, and by which I may measure actions, whether yours or those of any one else, and then I shall be able to say that such and such an action is pious, such another impious."[11] On and on went Euthyphro, and back came Socrates; until Euthyphro, having endured all the inner suffering he could stand, came to the conclusion that he had best be off to prosecute his father. Socrates ended his conversation with a word of discouragement. "Alas! my companion; and will you leave me in despair? I was hoping that you would instruct me in the nature of piety and impiety; and then I would have cleared myself of Meletus and his indictment. I would have told him that I had been enlightened by Euthyphro, and had given up rash innovations and speculations, in which I indulged only through ignorance, and that now I am about to lead a better life."[12]

Socrates did not succeed in converting many to strive for existential virtue, but this did not trouble Kierkegaard; for it

---

[8] *Euthyphro*, part 4.
[9] *Ibid.*, part 5.
[10] *Ibid.*, part 6.
[11] *Idem.*
[12] *Ibid.*, parts 15c-16.

was enough that the Athenian sage went at the problem of virtue in the right way. " 'The individual'; that category has only been used once before and then by Socrates, in a dialectical and decisive way, to disintegrate paganism."[13]

In the same spirit Kierkegaard undertook his assignment of trying to make people individuals. "There cannot really be the least doubt that what Christianity needs is another Socrates, someone who could existentially express ignorance with the same cunning dialectical simplicity, or as it should be said: I cannot understand the first thing about faith, but I believe. But it is all that understanding and conceiving which is the misfortune."[14]

The interesting feature of this is the manner in which Kierkegaard thought that a retreat from individual responsibility was a cardinal sin, though one which was never classified in the daily newspaper along with those sins which corrupt the virtue of the social order.

> Of all debauchery the cleverness of this corruption (pantheistic) is the most disgusting. A man may sin personally in his youth, seduce girls, take to drink — there is always the hope that it will one day strike his conscience as sin. But the respectability, the wretched brilliance of perdition, which surrounds the idea of the individual losing himself in the generation, confusing himself with Rome, Greece, and Asia, that mouldy form of conceit, ends in his not belonging to those who, physically speaking and with sensual rapture are *diliciis diffluentes* but intellectually speaking, in the stupidity of imbecility, are *diffluentes*.[15]

When an individual rejects his responsibility to mediate truth within the freedom of his own person, he pays a heavy price. The power which belongs to him is surrendered to the group, and he ends up as nothing but a number in an impersonal column.

> The crowd is composed of individuals, but it must also be in the power of each one to be what he is: an individual; and no one, no one at all, no one whatsoever is prevented from being an individual unless he prevents himself — by becoming

---

[13] Kierkegaard, *Journals*, 723.
[14] *Ibid.*, 733.
[15] *Ibid.*, 543.

one of the masses. To become one of the masses, to collect the masses around one is, on the contrary, what makes for differences in life; and even those who mean best may offend the individual by discussing the subject. And in that way the masses have the power once again, influence, recognition, dominion — and that too is the difference in life which, ruling, overlooks the individual as weak and powerless.[16]

Dreadful though this side of the price may be, there is yet a more dreadful side: the entertainment of a frivolous attitude toward God. It follows, therefore, that Kierkegaard's struggle to defend the individual is, in reality, a preparation for a defense of those responsibilities which the individual must undertake if he is to be a Christian in the true and proper sense.

B. *Making It Difficult To Be a Christian*

Kierkegaard was closer to the vocation of prophet than he was to the vocation of a missionary, for whereas a missionary seeks to bring the gospel to pagan tribes, a prophet has the thankless task of speaking *against* those of his own believing community — those who have become so complacent about the gospel that they no longer experience fear and trembling. A prophet, to be sure, *is* a kind of missionary. But he is a special kind, for he resorts to the category of "the individual."

> It is not the category which missionaries can use in dealing with heathens when they preach the Gospel, but the category of a missionary in Christianity itself, so as to make the change, which lies in being and becoming a Christian, a more inward change. When he comes the missionary will use that category. For if the age is waiting for a hero it waits in vain. It is far more probable that a man will come who will teach them obedience in divine weakness — by making them rebel against God by putting to death the one who was obedient to God.[17]

The motivation of this prophetic office came, in no small part, from the fear and trembling which Kierkegaard himself experienced as he sought to become a Christian, together with the distressing observation that those who were so quick to ridicule

---

[16] *Ibid.*, 614.
[17] *Ibid.*, 723.

him perceived no inward responsibility. And so it follows that even here, in the prophetic office, Kierkegaard was somewhat motivated by a subtle defense of himself as a Christian as well as an individual.

Kierkegaard's disgust with the complacency of those who professed to be Christians was but another side to his impatience with those who rested in Christianity as an objective system. "Under the guise of objectivity people have wished to sacrifice individualities completely. That is the whole question."[18] Without suggesting frivolity in spiritual matters, let us illustrate a case of objective mannerism, the type which so greatly disturbed Kierkegaard as he reflected on what it meant to become a Christian. Suppose a person is told that he is going to meet God. If the person fails to perceive that such a meeting calls for a serious act of repentance and humility on his part, in other words if he fails to feel his existential responsibility to be a Christian and an individual, he might reply in the following manner: "Oh, what a fortunate day for me! Not many people have the privilege of meeting God. I must hurry home for my camera. Then I shall get a haircut, as well as wear my best suit. I can't *wait* to meet God; it is sort of like meeting the president."

At this point there may be those who may complain that Kierkegaard is trying to have his cake and his penny, too; for it seems to be a violation of the law of consistency to say that the door to Christianity is opened when one settles for individuality, on the one hand, and then to turn right around and assume that one is discharging his individuality by making it difficult to become a Christian, on the other. Which is it?

The answer is, it is both. A dialectic is involved at this point, and dialectic implies a conflict between seemingly inharmonious points of view. Kierkegaard not only believed that an existential understanding of life conflicts at points with the requirements of strict logical inference, but in the event that a choice had to be made between the existential and the logical, Kierkegaard unhesitatingly chose the existential.

[18] *Ibid.*, 631.

Becoming an individual blends with the responsibility of becoming a Christian because a person does not succeed in becoming an individual until he realizes with his whole heart that he lives and moves and has his being in God — and not in God as a mere metaphysical entity, but in God as the heavenly person through whom one finds selfhood, and who discloses his person to this world through oneself.

> And how does a man become that individual? Well, unless he has to do with God alone, where the highest matters are concerned, and says: now I weigh the matter as best I can, act upon it that you, O God, may be able to seize hold of me, and I therefore speak to nobody at all, I dare not do so — unless he does that he cannot become the individual. The moment I talk to another man about my highest concerns, of what God wills for me, in that very moment God has less power over me. How many are there who are able to grasp God's priority of claim on a man, so that the permission to talk to another man about one's highest concerns is an indulgence, a concession which one must pray for, because no mere man can endure being an individual absolutely.[19]

Now, although Kierkegaard kept the affirmative goal before him of helping people become individuals and Christians, he concluded that the affirmative goal would best be reached by shocking people with a realization of how difficult it was to become a Christian. This paradox is perfectly expressed by the following brief conviction: *"it is easier to become a Christian when I am not a Christian than to become a Christian when I am one."*[20] In other words, the person who nurses the idea that he is a Christian because he has been baptized, or because he has memorized the catechism, or because he assents to the right theology — such a person must be shattered by a realization that becoming a Christian demands much more than correct form or formula.

This partly explains why Kierkegaard never composed a systematic theology. Such a species of writing (so Kierkegaard thought) would only have hindered people from becoming Christians, for a systematic theology can be memorized while a

---

[19] *Ibid.*, 1161.
[20] Kierkegaard, *Concluding Unscientific Postscript*, p. 327.

game of cards is being played. In such a situation the terms of Christianity become altogether painless, and Kierkegaard would have no part in this.[21]

And more than this, one searches in vain for a glossary of major terms. Not even the terms Christian and Christianity, though used over and over again, are formally defined for the reader. This was not due to a careless oversight. On the contrary, it was a deliberate strategy; for Kierkegaard was persuaded that any easy, objective definition of Christianity would edify no one. Even worse, it might turn out to be a stumbling-block in the way of a person's becoming a Christian; and it would do this by tempting such a person to presume that he was a Christian for the sheer reason that he was able to give an accurate definition of Christianity. Existential (living) responsibility must take priority in all spiritual relations.

> So far as my knowledge extends, there exists no definition of what seriousness is. I should be glad of this, if it be true; not because I am fond of the modern fluent way of thinking which has abolished definitions and lets everything coalesce, but because when it is a question of existential concepts it always is a sign of surer tact to abstain from definitions, because one does not like to construe in the form of a definition which so easily makes something else and something different out of a thought which essentially must be understood in a different fashion and which one has understood differently and has loved in an entirely different way.[22]

If it is a sign of boorishness for a bridegroom to postpone the wedding ceremonies until he is able to think through an objective definition of marital love, how much more is it boorishness to postpone surrender to God until an objective definition of love for God is thought through? Love, in both cases, can only be known through the inner experience of love, and such an experience comes into being through personal commitment.

---

[21] A word of caution must be injected here. Kierkegaard's books are very orderly. All we mean to imply is that the use of indirect communication prompted Kierkegaard to avoid coming right out and saying what he meant. He deliberately tried to make his readers *work* when they set out to read his books. And there is no doubt that he succeeded in reaching this goal.

[22] Kierkegaard, *The Concept of Dread*, pp. 130-131.

This brings into focus the oft-repeated assertion that Christianity is subjectivity. "Christianity is not a doctrine but an existential communication expressing an existential contradiction."[23]

Before we rush into a critique of Kierkegaard, however, let us pause to appreciate his feeling of grief that, as he presumed, the Copenhagen of his day was actually a pagan city which took refuge under the title of Christianity. In other words, he suspected that the citizens professed the Christian faith because it was fashionable and gave them social status — something like owning a new automobile or a new house that others envied. Kierkegaard not only felt a divine calling to do something about this situation, but he concluded that the best thing he could do was to clarify the reasons why it was difficult to become a Christian.

> My purpose is to make it difficult to become a Christian, yet not more difficult than it is, nor to make it difficult for stupid people, and easy for clever pates, but qualitatively difficult, and essentially difficult for every man equally, for essentially it is equally difficult for every man to relinquish his understanding and his thinking, and to keep his ' soul fixed upon the absurd. . . .[24]

Kierkegaard realized that he was engaged in the construction of a relation between eternity and time which would offend his generation, but he justified the necessity of such a construction by the way in which his generation had deliberately avoided the subjective responsibilities entailed in Christianity. "It is not my fault that the age in which we live has reversed the relationship, and transformed Christianity into a philosophical doctrine that asks to be understood, and turned *being* a Christian into a triviality. To assume that this denial that Christianity is a doctrine should imply that Christianity is contentless, is merely a *chicane*. When the believer exists in his faith his existence acquires tremendous content, but not in the sense of paragraph-material."[25]

Kierkegaard was willing to give his generation the benefit of

---

[23] Kierkegaard, *Concluding Unscientific Postscript*, p. 339.
[24] *Ibid.*, p. 495.
[25] *Ibid.*, pp. 339-340.

the doubt — that is, if there ever was an occasion for doubt. He constantly sought for quality, rather than quantity, when adding up the fruits of his and others' efforts to restore the true dignity of the Christian faith. Even "one single true Christian is enough to justify the assertion that Christianity exists."[26] But the more Kierkegaard became persuaded that personal complacency and the Christian ideal were being confused, the more he was forced to the conclusion that "Christianity simply does not exist."[27] Passion and sacrifice had been displaced by fashion and rote.

> The visible Church has suffered so broad an expansion that all the original relationships have been reversed. Just as it once required energy and determination to become a Christian, so now, though the renunciation be not praiseworthy, it requires courage and energy to renounce the Christian religion, while it needs only thoughtlessness to remain a nominal Christian.[28]

This shift from the intellectual task of teaching *what* Christianity is, to the existential task of proclaiming acceptance of Christianity as a responsible act, brought about in Protestantism what Swenson rather aptly describes as a "veritable Copernican revolution, one in my opinion infinitely more significant than the much heralded astronomical one, the same Copernican revolution which is effected in the soul of every man when he becomes mature in the consciousness that it is not so much he that cross-examines existence, as existence that cross-examines him."[29] By urging others to take inventory of their inward state before God, rather than reflect upon their intellectual compliance with Christianity as an objective system, Kierkegaard sincerely hoped that he would help others to make a transition from complacency to passionate concern, from nonchalance before God to holy fear and trembling.

It follows from this that the goal of science and the goal of Christianity stand at polar opposites — at least as Kierke-

---

[26] Kierkegaard, *Attack Upon "Christendom,"* p. 127. Princeton University Press, Princeton, 1946. Translated by Walter Lowrie.
[27] *Ibid.*, p. 277.
[28] Kierkegaard, *Concluding Unscientific Postscript*, p. 326.
[29] Swenson, *Something About Kierkegaard*, p. 126.

gaard understood them. While science seeks to reduce the personal element to absolute zero, Christianity seeks to reduce the impersonal element to absolute zero. "The difference between subjective and objective thinking must express itself also in the form of communication suitable to each."[30] Let us not pervert this, however, by suggesting that Kierkegaard had any objections to science as such. The point is that the formal, objective, mechanical, impersonal elements which make up scientific methodology are inappropriate when the methodology of becoming a Christian is in question.

Kierkegaard's purpose in making it difficult to become a Christian, or we may say, his purpose in stating Christianity as an either/or, was solely that of devising a means by which he could shock professing Christians out of their Laodicean state of lukewarmness.[31] He was convinced that wherever passionate, responsible decision was missing, both individuality and Christianity were also missing. "So then, better frank sincerity than lukewarmness."[32]

> His one concern was to present Christ to men in such a way as to search their hearts and lead them to decide for or against Him. He was an evangelist rather than a theologian. There can be no question about his own adherence to the orthodox Christian faith of the oecumenical creeds. But he sought to speak to the needs of the times rather than give a timeless exposition of the faith.[33]

As one searches the history of philosophy and the history of the philosophy of religion, no one — Socrates and Lessing notwithstanding — developed an existential methodology which was more compatible with Kierkegaard's than Blaise Pascal. To begin with, Pascal seemed to have had grave reservations about the ability of reason to close the gap between time and eternity. "Reason, therefore, ends in doubt and leaves us in the lurch

---

[30] Kierkegaard, *Concluding Unscientific Postscript*, p. 68.
[31] Revelation 3:14-22.
[32] Kierkegaard, *op. cit.*, p. 521.
[33] Denzil G. M. Patrick, *Pascal and Kierkegaard, A Study in the Strategy of Evangelism*, II, p. 306.

when it comes to our deepest interests."[34] God is not a person whom we can examine objectively; he is a hidden God: *Deus absconditus*.[35] Still, the matters pertaining to the soul and its eternal destiny are so important that they must be given first place in our scale of values. "All our actions and thoughts must take such different courses, according as there are or are not eternal joys to hope for, that it is impossible to take one step with sense and judgment unless we regulate our course by our view of this point which ought to be our ultimate end."[36] Even though we are ignorant of what forms the essence of our body, soul, and the universe, "nothing is so important to man as his own state, nothing is so formidable to him as eternity . . . ."[37] Since our life is but a passing vapor, and since eternity is forever, we must passionately cast ourselves on the things which pertain to eternity. Still, some may ask, Why should we do this? Pascal says we *must* do it, that is all there is to it. But what if a person shrinks from this passionate commitment, demanding suitable evidence before action is taken one way or another? Pascal replies:

> Yes; but you must wager. It is not optional. You are embarked. Which will you choose then? Let us see. Since you must choose, let us see which interests you least. You have two things to lose, the true and the good; and two things to stake, your reason and your will, your knowledge and your happiness; and your nature has two things to shun, error and misery. Your reason is no more shocked in choosing one rather than the other, since you must of necessity choose. This is one point settled. But your happiness? Let us weigh the gain and the loss in wagering that God is. Let us estimate these two chances. If you gain, you gain all; and if you lose, you lose nothing. Wager, then, without hesitation that He is.[38]

There is no way to establish a causal connection between Pascal and Kierkegaard, for Kierkegaard mentions very little

---

[34] Frank Thilly, *A History of Philosophy*, p. 291. Henry Holt and Company, New York, 1914.
[35] Cf. passages in the Bible such as Isaiah 45:15: "Truly, thou art a God who hidest thyself. . . . "
[36] Pascal, *Pensées*, Section III.
[37] *Idem.*
[38] *Idem.*

about Pascal in his books. Nonetheless, both men were engaged in the common task of attacking existing forms of Christianity, as well as enriching faith by a defense of inner passion. "The reason for his [Kierkegaard's] conflict with the established order was precisely the same as the reason for Pascal's conflict with the Jesuits: both men took absolutely seriously the unconditional demands of the Gospel, and could not bear to see them minimized or explained away for reasons of convenience or expediency."[39] Even though Pascal tended to assign a higher place to reason than Kierkegaard would concede, both philosophers of religion shared a common purpose: "to affirm the absolute contradictions in human life in such a way as to lead men to seek refuge from despair in Jesus Christ and experience His life-transforming power."[40]

C. *Disclosing the Role of the Witness*

Although the maieutic stage aptly served the purpose for which it was introduced, it was neither the last nor the highest stage through which Kierkegaard passed as he tried to relieve himself of his inner burden.

> The communication of Christianity must ultimately end in "bearing witness", the maieutic form can never be final. For truth, from the Christian point of view, does not lie in the subject (as Socrates understood it) but in a revelation which must be proclaimed. In Christendom the maieutic form can certainly be used, simply because the majority in fact live under the impression that they are Christians. But since Christianity is Christianity the maieuticer must become the witness. In the end the maieuticer will not be able to bear the responsibility because the indirect method is ultimately rooted in human intelligence, however much it may be sanctified and consecrated by fear and trembling. God becomes too powerful for the maieuticer and so he is the witness, though different from the direct witness in that he has been through the process of becoming one.[41]

The maieutic stage was one of growth and transition. It served a needed purpose when Kierkegaard, overwhelmed by a melan-

---
[39] Patrick, *op. cit.*, pp. 320-321.
[40] *Ibid.*, p. 322.
[41] Kierkegaard, *Journals*, 809.

choly and dread which grew out of the feeling that he was nothing but a wretched skeptic searching for truth, took refuge under pseudonyms. But growth in courage was accompanied by growth in insight. "For many years my melancholy has prevented me from being on terms of real intimacy with myself. In between my melancholy and myself lay a whole world of the imagination. That is, in part, what I rid myself of in the pseudonyms."[42]

The expedient of indirect communication is negatively aimed at exposing the false complacency of those who claim that Christianity is merely a theological system to which one gives intellectual assent. But since the true glory of Christianity lies in revelation, and especially the daily revelation which an individual makes when he existentially or in a passionate, living way mediates the essence of eternity, Kierkegaard concluded that he would fall short of the mark unless he not only disclosed the role of the witness, but unless he himself fulfilled this role in his own life. As Kierkegaard perceived the picture in Christianity, a witness ranked above a teacher when it came to the art of proclaiming the meaning of Christianity. "What is a witness? A witness is a man who immediately supplies proof of the truth of the doctrine he is proclaiming — immediately, well, partly by there being truth in him and blessedness, partly at once offering himself and saying: see now whether you can compel me to deny this doctrine."[43]

It was only because Kierkegaard understood that it was necessary to *be* a Christian in daily actions that he was able to compose such a masterpiece on Christian ethics as *Works of Love*. To love after the manner of Jesus Christ *is* the essence of witnessing, and the act is living proof that the meaning of Christianity is understood: ". . . an understanding of the truth belongs to being a witness to the truth. . . ."[44]

Kierkegaard did not turn to the role of a witness merely to augment the sense of peace in his own heart. He also wanted to serve as a helpful, constructive partner to those who, shat-

---

[42] *Ibid.*, 641.
[43] *Ibid.*, 1091.
[44] *Ibid.*, 1280.

tered by their realization that they had to assume the responsibility of *being* Christians, were not altogether sure how to go about this responsibility. It is one thing to deflate complacent Christians; it is another thing to take them by the hand and lead them into green pastures of truth and righteousness. "People will make it appear that I wanted to introduce pietism, little, pusillanimous self-abnegations in matters of no consequence. No thank you, I never wanted that in the very slightest degree. What I want is to spur people on to becoming moral characters, witnesses to the truth, to be willing to suffer for the truth, and ready to give up worldly wisdom."[45]

Kierkegaard fell into a pit of great difficulty, however, when he attempted to correlate his position with the traditional Christian presuppositions that God the Father is a person and that Jesus Christ is His Son. He was satisfied to speak of God the Father as pure activity *(actus purus)*,[46] though he made no systematic effort to explain how a being characterized by pure activity can either reveal himself or have an interest in the flux of temporal affairs. But in the case of Jesus Christ, the Son of God, Kierkegaard was forced to reintroduce the concept of indirect communication; although in this instance the indirect communication was not merely a *literary* expedient. It was part and parcel of the means by which God stimulates *faith* in individuals.

> Such is the case with the God-Man. . . . When one says directly, "I am God; the Father and I are one", that is direct communication. But when he who says it is an individual man, quite like other men, then this communication is not just perfectly direct; for it is not just perfectly clear and direct that an individual man should be God — although what he says is perfectly direct. By reason of the communicator the communication contains a contradiction, it becomes indirect communication, it puts to thee a choice, whether thou wilt believe Him or not.[47]

[45] *Ibid.*, 1138.
[46] *Absolute and unsullied love,* that is.
[47] Kierkgaard, *Training in Christianity,* p. 134. Princeton University Press, Princeton, 1947. Translated by Walter Lowrie.

Chapter Three

KIERKEGAARD'S VIEW OF MAN

SINCE KIERKEGAARD STROVE SO HARD TO TELL WHAT IT MEANT to be an individual and a Christian, it is not surprising that he also gave a good deal of attention to the nature of man. He did not consider such a question an end in itself, of course. Rather, he used it as an additional means by which he could more firmly establish his conviction that the most important responsibility in life *is* that of being an individual and a Christian.

At this point we must concentrate on select portions in *The Concept of Dread*, for here Kierkegaard developed his view of man by a unique appeal to two complementary syntheses. We shall refer to these as "Synthesis A" and "Synthesis B."

It is extremely important, however, that we keep Kierkegaard's basic methodology before us, lest we make the mistake of thinking that the two syntheses were introduced to describe an objective or ontological view of man. Kierkegaard deliberately interpreted man *functionally* or *existentially*. In this way — so he thought — he avoided the complaint that he was merely another armchair philosopher.

A. Synthesis A

Kierkegaard wasted no words in defining what he meant by the first synthesis in man. "Everything turns upon dread coming into view. Man is a synthesis of the soulish and the bodily. But a synthesis is unthinkable if the two are not united in a third factor. This third factor is the spirit."[1] Let us now examine this synthesis, considering the body first.

There is no reason to belabor the point that man is body, for whoever denies this must use parts of his body — tongue, hands, head, etc. — thus witnessing to the very fact that he is trying so hard to deny.[2]

Actually, the important role which body fills has encouraged materialists in all ages to draw the conclusion that *all* of man is nothing but a highly complex physical organism which is only distinguished from the rest of nature by the fact that the laws which govern human consciousness are more mysterious than those found in the animal kingdom.

Kierkegaard would rightly respond that *freedom* is the critical point of distinction between man and animal; and by freedom he would intend primarily man's capacity to make correct ethical choices.

Socrates composed a very devastating argument against materialism. In the dialogue, *Phaedo,* the venerable Socrates tells Cebes how thrilled he was when, weary of materialism, he read that Anaxagoras introduced the principle of *nous* (mind or reason) as the disposer and cause of all. But the Socratic thrill soon ebbed away, for the principle of mind in the philosophy of Anaxagoras turned out to be nothing but another eccentricity of matter. It was in no sense a principle of moral

---

[1] Kierkegaard, *The Concept of Dread,* p. 39.

[2] Since I have felt that the methodology of existentialism has all too often been left standing without a firm foundation beneath it, I have tried to develop an epistemology (theory of knowledge) to help provide such a foundation. This epistemology, which has much in common with the views of both Socrates and Kierkegaard, appeals to the realities which already hold a person by reason of existence itself. See my volume, *Christian Commitment,* Macmillan, 1957 (now distributed by the Wm. B. Eerdmans Publishing Co.). Check the index for those sections of the volume where "the third method of knowing" is developed.

and rational freedom which sat in judgment over matter. This disappointment provided Socrates with a perfect occasion to develop an existential proof that man is more than body.

> I might compare him [Anaxagoras] to a person who began by maintaining generally that mind is the cause of the actions of Socrates, but who, when he endeavored to explain the causes of my several actions in detail, went on to show that I sit here [condemned] because my body is made up of bones and muscles; and the bones, as he would say, are hard and have joints which divide them, and the muscles are elastic, and they cover the bones, which have also a covering or environment of flesh and skin which contains them; and as the bones are lifted at their joints by the contraction or relaxation of the muscles, I am able to bend my limbs, and this is why I am sitting here in a curved posture — that is what he would say; and he would have a similar explanation of my talking to you, which he would attribute to sound, and air, and hearing, and he would assign ten thousand other causes of the same sort, forgetting to mention the true cause, which is, that the Athenians have thought fit to condemn me, and accordingly I have thought it better and more right to remain here and undergo my sentence; for I am inclined to think that these muscles and bones of mine would have gone off long ago to Megara or Boeotia — by the dog, they would, if they had been moved only by their own idea of what was best, and if I had not chosen the better and nobler part, instead of playing truant and running away, of enduring any punishment which the state inflicts.[3]

Since the logic of Socrates cannot be meaningfully refuted, one is forced to conclude that man, functionally understood, is soul as well as body. Man is free to accept or reject alternatives; hence, he cannot be wholly explained by purely physical criteria.

Man as soul (if we may speak in this manner without implying that Kierkegaard had any intention to defend an objective trichotomy) is that animating faculty — generally known by its association with free conduct — which separates living creatures from pure matter. Iron is iron; it has no power of contrary choice. But man and higher animals *can* make choices. Both are free to go to the left or to the right — other things being equal, of course.

[3] Plato, *Phaedo,* 98b-99a.

But have we yet addressed ourselves to that which makes the human species unique? Those who rush forward to answer this in the affirmative remain blind, says Kierkegaard, to the moral qualities in a man which make it possible for *him*, in contrast to a higher animal, to be an individual and a Christian — conscience, an intuition of personal dignity, etc.

> It is really the conscience which constitutes a personality. Personality is an individual decision, substantiated by being known to God in the possibility of the conscience. For the conscience may slumber, but the constitutive factor is its possibility. Otherwise the decision would be a transitory fact. Nor is the consciousness of the decision, self-consciousness, the constitutive factor, in so far as that is merely the relation within which the decision is related to itself, whereas the co-knowledge of God is the determining factor, the confirmation.[4]

The role played by *spirit* is crucial to Kierkegaard's understanding of that dialectic and creative activity which is so characteristic of a living man. Neither true individuality nor true Christianity would exist apart from the either/or dimension of spirit. "Man's essential idea is spirit, and we must not permit ourselves to be confused by the fact that he is also able to walk on two legs. The idea in language is thought, and we must not permit ourselves to be disturbed by the opinion of certain sentimental people, that its highest significance is to produce inarticulate sounds."[5] As we have already observed, higher animals are free to decide whether to go to the left or to the right; but only man enjoys spiritual freedom to make both God and man's relation to God the objects of passionate concern.

While spirit frequently works in and through soul, it is not the same as soul. Spirit makes it possible for man to experience personal transformation by a shift of ethical *possibility* into ethical *being*. Thus, if body and soul go far in explaining the

---

[4] Kierkegaard, *Journals*, 560. In his enthusiasm to link conscience with personality, Kierkegaard failed to place a proper emphasis upon what I call "the judicial sentiment." Again, see my volume, *Christian Commitment*.

[5] Kierkegaard, *Either/Or*, I, 52. Princeton University Press, Princeton, 1946. Translated by Walter Lowrie.

descriptive essence of man, spirit goes far in explaining the *imperative* essence.

Reinhold Niebuhr eloquently speaks of spirit as that expression of freedom which makes it possible for man to stand "outside of nature, life, himself, his reason and the world. This latter fact is appreciated in one or the other of its aspects by various philosophies. But it is not frequently appreciated in its total import."[6] Again,

> How difficult it is to do justice to both the uniqueness of man and his affinities with the world of nature below him is proved by the almost unvarying tendency of those philosophies, which describe and emphasize the rational faculties of man or his capacity for self-transcendence, to forget his relation to nature and to identify him, prematurely and unqualifiedly, with the divine and the eternal; and of naturalistic philosophies to obscure the uniqueness of man.[7]

Thus, the real point to "Synthesis A" will elude us unless we inwardly and passionately come to terms with the truth — so aptly stated by Niebuhr — that man is a problem unto himself. Man is a creature who is limited by nature, and yet who is rationally and spiritually free to stand outside this limitation by imagining possibilities which terminate in eternity. Nonetheless, as both Kierkegaard and Niebuhr realized, it is extremely difficult to maintain a satisfactory balance between necessity and possibility.

B. *Synthesis B*

The second synthesis has a baffling quality about it, for in strictest terms it doesn't seem to be a synthesis at all. But the more anxious we become, the more delighted Kierkegaard becomes, for anxiety is one of the subtle expedients by which he hopes to draw fresh attention to what he is saying.

> As for the latter synthesis, it evidently is not fashioned in the same way as the former. In the former case the two factors were soul and body, and the spirit was a third term, but was a

---

[6] Reinhold Niebuhr, *The Nature and Destiny of Man*, I, 3-4. Charles Scribner's Sons, New York, 1946.
[7] *Ibid.*, p. 4.

> third term in such a sense that there could not properly be any question of a synthesis until the spirit was posited. The other synthesis has only two factors: the temporal and the eternal. Where is the third term? And if there be no third term, there is really no synthesis; for a synthesis of that which is a contradiction cannot be completed as a synthesis without a third term, for the recognition that the synthesis is a contradiction is precisely the assertion that it is not a synthesis. What then is the temporal?[8]

When all is said and done, it seems that the first synthesis describes man as a creature who is simultaneously free and involved, while the second synthesis describes man as a creature who has functional power to unite eternity in time. It turns out, therefore, that these two syntheses are actually *one* synthesis described in two different ways. Kierkegaard, of course, does not suffer the slightest worry that he is confusing his reader by indulging in what seems to be nothing but a melody of words, for he feels he is exercising a privilege to which one is rightly entitled when he approaches the nature of man functionally and existentially, rather than scientifically or objectively.

> The synthesis of the eternal and the temporal is not a second synthesis but is the expression for the first synthesis in consequence of which man is a synthesis of soul and body sustained by spirit. No sooner is the spirit posited than the instant is there. For this reason it can be said reproachfully of man that he lives only in the instant, since this comes about by an arbitrary abstraction. Nature does not lie in the instant.[9]

It is quite fair, however, to ask *how* the human species manages to mediate eternity in time. We need more than a melody of words to solve this problem.

If a secular philosopher acknowledges the operation of *mind* in man, but not the operation of *spirit,* he will, of course, sense no problem at all. As for the mediation of eternity in time — if there is any justification for speaking of such mediation in the first place — it need consist of nothing more than the painless act of thinking. This is a routine accomplishment and merits no special attention.

---

[8] Kierkegaard, *The Concept of Dread*, p. 76.
[9] *Ibid.,* p. 79.

Kierkegaard, quite naturally, has little patience with such an impersonal, objective approach to man. He is determined to speak about man only when he himself is deeply involved as a man. This means that man is not properly understood until he is approached as a creature who has the existential responsibility of mediating eternity in time; *i.e.*, unless he is approached as one who must give concrete, daily existence to that which, perceived by spirit, antecedently exists in eternity.

A secular philosopher — if consistent — will avoid the admission of anything existential in man. He makes sure that there is no connection between himself as a person and the theories developed by his intellect.

Kierkegaard's emphasis on the role of spirit gives us a very helpful introduction to the meaning of what he repeatedly calls, "Truth is subjectivity." The eternal, as ethically perceived, is brought into time whenever a concerned human being undertakes the task of existence so seriously that his very selfhood is at stake. In other words, truth becomes part of the subject whenever the subject wholeheartedly wills to *be* the truth.

It now ought to be plain why "Synthesis B" is deliberately stated in a somewhat confusing manner. Kierkegaard aimed at catapulting man into such a predicament that man would take responsible, spiritual steps to complete his own being. Thus, though the term "spirit" is admittedly used in a rather loose way at times, its central purpose is to emphasize both the heights and responsibility of human freedom; and such freedom, when properly understood, implies the necessity of personal, ethical choice. In other words, whenever the whole self is wholly committed to the task of *being* a whole self, the mediation of eternity in time results. Spirit soars into the substance of the ethical imperative. Then, with authorization from the self as it realizes that the very being of the self is at stake, it seizes the right hand of eternity and joins it with the right hand of time — though functionally and existentially, let us remember, and not ontologically or metaphysically.

Disturbed readers may wonder if Kierkegaard's total dedication to the subjective character of truth has not led him to the place where it may sometimes be more praiseworthy to become inwardly passionate over the claims of objective *error* than to remain inwardly calm before the claims of objective *truth*. The following admission of Kierkegaard seems to support this type of concern:

> Spirituality is: the power of a man's understanding over his life. The man who, with a perhaps false idea of God, nevertheless follows out the self-denial which that false idea demands of him, is more spiritual than the man who, in learning and philosophy, has a correct knowledge of God, but upon whose life it has no power whatsoever.[10]

Let us agree, however, to postpone our evaluation until we have given Kierkegaard a full opportunity to spell out the criteria to which he appeals when he attempts to validate his subjective approach to truth.

In any event, we are clearly told that spirit succeeds in uniting the first two elements in the second synthesis — the eternal and the temporal — by operating in and through what Kierkegaard describes as "the instant."

> Thus understood, the instant ['a glance of the eye,' in other words] is not properly an atom of time but an atom of eternity. It is the finite reflection of eternity in time, its first effort as it were to bring time to a stop. . . . The instant is that ambiguous moment in which time and eternity touch one another, thereby positing *the temporal,* where time is constantly intersecting eternity and eternity constantly permeating time.[11]

Eternity, though fragmented into atomic particles, does not become man's rightful possession until man vehemently and ethically *decides* for the eternal in time.

With this before us it is relevant that we look once again at Kierkegaard's heated rejection of the concept of immanence. Reference to the vocation of Socrates may help us at this point. Socrates, as he is portrayed by Kierkegaard, is an extraordinary person; he towered above others because he had both the wisdom and the courage to associate the *true* individual with the *existing* individual. But he didn't complete his course, for he continued to nurse the tacit expectation that a person who used his head

---

[10] *Journals,* 1177.
[11] Kierkegaard, *The Concept of Dread,* pp. 79-80.

correctly would meet the requirements of existence by the sheer act of recollection. In sum: though Socrates was impatient with irrelevant speculation, he nonetheless assumed that the rational man, by a disciplined exercise of his powers of recollection, could once again experience the union with eternity which he previously knew before that cursed day when he was imprisoned within the limits of a body. It would seem, then, that Socrates failed to appreciate the *spiritual* faculty in man.

Immanence, let us remember, expresses the conviction that man is so similar to God, or God is so similar to man, that a thinking individual can exercise his highest faculty by merely defining eternal truth in a detached, objective manner. Kierkegaard, however, was convinced that immanence would only encourage people to lie on a hammock and yawn in conceit, for why should a person become passionately and ethically excited about a state which necessarily exists? If immanence is true, man is continuous with eternity whether he does anything about it or not.

It now begins to appear that Kierkegaard was so revolted by the threat of immanence that he deliberately constructed his two syntheses in order to help man realize that he had a personal responsibility to mediate the eternal in time. In short, the very *being* of man was at stake. This interpretation of life could not be taken lightly — not unless one had become blinded as a result of resting in the claims of immanence.

At this point we can strengthen our approach by noting the special role which Kierkegaard assigned to objective paradox. It is safe to say that man, in his estimation, would not be fully shaken out of his complacency until the notion of a peaceful, compatible link between man and God was altogether shattered; and paradox seemed to be ideally suited to carry out this task — so Kierkegaard presumed, at least.

> If it was paradoxical to posit the eternal truth in relationship to an existing individual, it is now absolutely paradoxical to posit it in relationship to such an individual as we have here defined. But the more difficult it is made for him to take himself out of existence by way of recollection, the more profound is the inwardness that his existence may have in existence; and when it is made impossible for him, when he is held so fast in existence

that the back door of recollection is forever closed to him, then his inwardness will be the most profound possible . . . . there can be no stronger expression for inwardness than when the retreat out of existence into the eternal by way of recollection is impossible; and when, with truth confronting the individual as a paradox, gripped in the anguish and pain of sin, facing the tremendous risk of the objective insecurity, the individual believes.[12]

Personally pleased with his two-sided conviction — (a) that unless a human being is confronted by objective paradox, (b) he will never be goaded on to become an individual and a Christian — Kierkegaard himself tended to drift toward what gives every evidence of being an expression of the very complacency which he so fiercely despised. For example, though he apparently felt no theological responsibility to explain *why* Jesus Christ was exempt from the task of mediating eternity through the common instant, Kierkegaard marched boldly forward and declared that there was an absolute instant in history when the eternal God clothed himself with the limitations of human nature. Presumably this Christological dogmatism was introduced to help undergird the apologetic ministry of paradox, for where could one find a more shocking paradox than that which forms the incarnation? "Behold where he stands — God! Where? There; do you not see him? He is God; and yet he has not a resting-place for his head, and he dares not lean on any man lest he cause him to be offended. He is God; and yet he picks his steps more carefully than if angels guided them, not to prevent his foot from stumbling against a stone, but lest he trample human beings in the dust, in that they are offended in him."[13]

Kierkegaard's delight with paradox, it seems, is really an extension of his rejection of immanence. Christianity is supposed to be taken seriously because it posits an absolute gulf between God and man. Fellowship with God cannot become a reality until God, by his grace, takes the initiative and enters time. Thus, the incarnation is an indictment of that conceit in human

---

[12] Kierkegaard, *Concluding Unscientific Postscript*, pp. 186-188. Once again it seems that Kierkegaard is on a collision course. But we shall examine this possibility at a later time.

[13] Kierkegaard, *Philosophical Fragments*, p. 25.

nature which imagines that man can close the gap between time and eternity by rationally moving upward.

C. Concluding Inferences

Once Kierkegaard's view of man has been at least partially understood, it is safe to assume that an increased appreciation of his vocation will also be experienced. The postulation of the two syntheses may seem overly academic, but all Kierkegaard sought was to prod man into a more conscientious acceptance of the role of being an individual and a Christian. Or we can state the same point a bit differently by the reminder that Kierkegaard was basically concerned with the ingredients which actually make up *existence*. Thus, authentic existence is a living condition in which spirit, having soared to eternity, arouses man to such a state of ethical and passionate decision that the atoms of eternity are mediated in time instant after instant.

> Existence is the child that is born of the infinite and the finite, the eternal and the temporal, and is therefore a constant striving . . . . or to say the same thing in other words, the thinking subject is an existing individual. It is only systematists and objective philosophers who have ceased to be human beings, and have become speculative philosophy in the abstract, an entity which belongs in the realm of pure being.[14]

It turns out, when all is said and done, that eternity is merely Kierkegaard's way of summing up man's outer spiritual and ethical possibilities. The more these possibilities are transformed into actualities through passionate decision, the more genuine a person becomes and the more he verifies the judgment that "Truth is subjectivity."

True humanity, however — when existentially expressed — is actually something which comes and goes. It comes when the terms of eternity are met in time, and it goes when they are not. Therefore, no person can boast that he has done all that is required of him, even though a habit of spirituality *does* contribute something to the ongoing work of sanctification.

[14] Kierkegaard, *Concluding Unscientific Postscript*, p. 85.

". . . the experience of choosing imparts to a man's nature a solemnity, a quiet dignity, which never is entirely lost."[15]

Reinhold Niebuhr, once again taking his cue from Kierkegaard, locates the heart of the Christian wisdom in the dialectic which emerges as man is suspended between creative possibilities as a free spirit, on the one hand, and the contingencies and necessities which make up the stuff of temporal existence, on the other. At this point the similarity of Niebuhr and Kierkegaard is plain, for both seem to tell the same story. Man is beckoned to rise to eternity through spirit; but man, in his whole self, proves to be too earth-bound to make such a journey.

Kierkegaard realizes that this is a dreadful predicament to be in. Yet, through a surprising move, he reverses the field and interprets the predicament as an occasion for the exercise of personal hope.

> Rightly understood, the eternal assigns only a little portion at a time in the possibility. Eternity is through the possible always *near* enough at hand, and yet *far* enough away to keep a man moving forward, progressing, toward the eternal. Thus eternity draws and lures man by the possibility from the cradle to the grave, if he will but choose to hope. . . . The possibility is equally as severe, or can be equally severe, as it can be gentle. Hope does not lie as a matter of course in the possibility, for fear may also lie in it. But the one who chooses hope, him the possibility, by the aid of hope, teaches to hope. Still the possibility of fear, the severity, remains, secretly present as a possibility, if it should be needed for the sake of education, for the purpose of arousing; but it remains hidden, while the eternal allures by the aid of hope. For the alluring always consists in being equally as *near* as *far away,* whereby the hopeful one is always kept hoping, hoping everything, preserved in hope for the eternal, which in the temporal existence is the possible.[16]

Whenever hope is active, spirit is also active. And the more genuinely spirit is active, the more the attributes of love are fulfilled, for love *is* the true mediating element between eternity

---

[15] Kierkegaard, *Either/Or,* II, 149.
[16] Kierkegaard, *Works of Love* p. 204.   Princeton University Press, Princeton, 1946. Translated by David F. Swenson and Lillian Marvin Swenson.

and time. Spirit, in other words, fills the instant (an atom of eternity) with works of love.

> What is it which connects the temporal and the eternal, what except love, which just for this reason is before everything, and which abides when everything else is past? But precisely because love is the bond of eternal, and because the temporal existence and eternity are heterogeneous, for that reason love may sometimes seem burdensome to the earthly prudence of the temporal existence, and therefore in this existence it may seem a tremendous relief to the sensual man to cast off this bond of the eternal.[17]

Although the genius of Kierkegaard permeates his writings everywhere, it is safe to assert that at no point is this genius more manifest than when he eloquently and biblically details the anatomy of spirit in *Works of Love*. If he had written no other book, surely the Danish gadfly would have earned a fixed position in the company of great authors.

In sum, whenever a human being rejects the responsibilities of love, he becomes spiritless; and being spiritless, he is only a potential person, for he has failed to complete the synthesis which forms the substance of genuine selfhood — *i.e.*, he has not taken seriously his God-given duty to mediate the absolute quality of eternity in the relativity of time. Such a human being continues to occupy space on this planet, to be sure, but this does not make him either an individual or a Christian. Unless spirit rises to its true heights, potentiality does not convert to actuality.

[17] *Ibid.*, p. 6.

Chapter Four

THE DIALECTIC OF INWARDNESS

IF TRUTH IS SUBJECTIVITY — A CONDITION OF PASSIONATE, ETHICAL inwardness which involves the very being or non-being of the whole self — then it follows, or so it would seem, that the more enthusiastically one decides to *be,* the more perfectly he *becomes* truth.

With this kind of inference heading his arsenal of thoughts, and also with many personal experiences to draw on, Kierkegaard studiously composed what we may call a "dialectic of inwardness." The purpose of such a dialectic was to help one gauge his location within the "stages"[1] on life's way. "There are three stages: an aesthetic, an ethical, and a religious. But these are not distinguished abstractly, as the immediate, the mediate and the synthesis of the two, but rather concretely, in existential determinations, as enjoyment-perdition; action-victory; suffering."[2] Again, "All interpretations of existence rank in ac-

---

[1] Lowrie convincingly points out that the concept of "stages" would be more effectively translated as "spheres" or, as Kierkegaard himself at times preferred, "existence-spheres."

[2] Kierkegaard, *Concluding Unscientific Postscript,* p. 261.

cordance with the degree of the individual's dialectical apprehension of inwardness."³

> There are three existence-spheres: the aesthetic, the ethical, the religious. The metaphysical is abstraction, there is no man who exists metaphysically. The metaphysical, ontology, *is* but it does not *exist;* for when it exists it is in the aesthetic, in the ethical, in the religious, and when it *is* it is the abstraction of or the *prius* for the aesthetic, the ethical, the religious. The ethical sphere is only a transitional sphere, and hence its highest expression is repentance as a negative action. The aesthetic sphere is that of immediacy, the ethical that of requirement (and this requirement is so infinite that the individual always goes bankrupt), the religious sphere is that of fulfilment, but note, not such a fulfilment as when one fills a cane or a bag with gold, for repentance has made infinite room, and hence the religious contradiction. . . .⁴

If Kierkegaard had been more consistent in the development of his methodology, however, he would have acknowledged only *two* "existence-spheres," for sub-ethical decisions are actually too trivial to rank. Sub-ethical decisions are *not* formed of either/or choices involving good and bad possibilities; yet without the passion which motivates such choices, no existential transformation is experienced.

A. *Boundaries Between the Stages*

Since the stages partially overlap, the boundaries which separate them are not absolutely distinct. "There are thus three spheres of existence: the aesthetic, the ethical, the religious. Two boundary zones correspond to these three: irony, constituting the boundary between the aesthetic and the ethical; humor, as the boundary that separates the ethical from the religious."⁵

Irony — which Socrates put to such cutting use — comes into being when finitude and the ethical task are set beside each other, thus suggesting a decisive contradiction.⁶

---

3 *Ibid.*, p. 506.
4 Kierkegaard, *Stages on Life's Way*, p. 430.
5 Kierkegaard, *Concluding Unscientific Postscript*, p. 448.
6 "Irony arises from the constant placing of the particularities of the finite together with the infinite ethical requirement, thus permitting the contradiction to come into being." *Idem.*

> Irony is a synthesis of ethical passion which infinitely accentuates inwardly the person of the individual in relation to the ethical requirement — and of culture, which infinitely abstracts externally from the personal ego, as one finitude among all the other finitudes and particularities. This abstraction causes the emphasis in the first attitude to pass unnoticed, and herein lies the art of the ironist, which also insures that the first movement shall be truly infinite. . . . But why does the ethicist use irony as his incognito? Because he grasps the contradiction there is between the manner in which he exists inwardly, and the fact that he does not outwardly express it. For the ethicist does indeed reveal himself, in so far as he pours himself forth in the tasks of the factual reality in which he lives; but this is something that the immediate individual also does, and what makes him an ethicist is the movement of the spirit by which he sets his outward life inwardly in juxtaposition with the infinite requirement of the ethical and this is something that is not directly apparent.[7]

Since humor is also a by-product of incongruous situations, it is not essentially different from irony. In any event, it arises when the self becomes sensitive to the manner in which the self offends its own ethical ideals. It requires considerable courage for a man to smile at himself under these conditions. Still, the genuineness of such humor — or perhaps its true role as a boundary between the ethical and the religious stages — is measured by the spiritual *pain* it occasions, and not by the width of the grin on one's face or by any other external.

> The different existential stages take rank in accordance with their relationship to the comical, depending on whether they have the comical within themselves or outside themselves; yet not in the sense that the comical is the highest stage. The immediate consciousness has the comical outside itself, for wherever there is life there is contradiction, but the contradiction is not represented in the immediate consciousness, which therefore has the contradiction coming from the outside. A finite worldly wisdom presumes to apprehend immediacy as comical, but thereby itself becomes comical; for the supposed justification of its comic apprehension is that it definitely knows the way out, but the way out which it knows is still more comical. This, then, is an illegitimate comic apprehension. Wherever

[7] *Ibid.*, pp. 449-450.

there exists a contradiction and the way out is not known, where the contradiction is not cancelled and corrected in something higher, there the contradiction is not painless; and where the contradiction is based on something only chimerically higher (from the frying-pan into the fire), it is itself still more comical, because the contradiction is greater. Thus in the relationship between immediacy and finite worldly wisdom. A comic apprehension on the basis of despair is also illegitimate, for despair is despair because it does not know the way out, does not know the contradiction cancelled, and ought therefore to apprehend the contradiction tragically, which is precisely the way to its healing.[8]

Relevant humor, therefore, surpasses irony because it involves a more intense perception of the self's existential guilt when the self is faced with ethical demands.

But such humor, despite its *nearness* to the religious life, may not be identified with such a life. Smiling at personal incongruity is hardly the same as inwardly repenting.

It follows, then, that the one who grasps the contradiction of existence and somehow manages to rally courage to smile at himself, is not far from the kingdom. But he is far enough away to be a cause for concern, for whoever resorts to laughter as an escape from the pain of repentance is following a course which is remarkably similar to that followed by non-Christians.

> Apparently, humor gives to existence a greater significance than irony does, but the immanent is predominant, and the more or less is a vanishing quantitative determination over against the qualitative decisiveness of the Christian position. Humor therefore becomes the last *terminus a quo* in connection with the problem of determining the Christian. When humor uses the Christian terminology (sin, the forgiveness of sins, atonement, God in time, etc.) it is not Christianity, but a pagan speculation which has acquired a *knowledge* of the Christian ideas. It can come deceptively close to the Christian position; but where decisiveness takes hold; where existence captures the existing individual so that he must remain in existence, while the bridge of immanence and recollection is burned behind him; where the decision comes to be in the moment, and the movement is forward

---

[8] *Ibid.*, pp. 463-464.

toward a relationship with the eternal truth which came into being in time: there humor does not follow.[9]

The humorist lacks the qualitative decisiveness which is necessary to *be*. He is almost an individual and a Christian — existentially speaking — but the "almost" merely adds to his tragedy.

B. *The Aesthetic Stage*

When Kierkegaard developed his philosophy of aestheticism, he used such a variety of approaches that some readers may be tempted to give up in despair. But any such despair is premature — provided we are willing to make serious use of what is recognized as a basic rule in hermeneutics: namely, that the later, more systematic works of a writer are a better index to his thinking than earlier or less systematic works. Thus, at this point in our effort to state the burden of Sören Kierkegaard, we shall rely mainly on what is Kierkegaard's greatest philosophic masterpiece, the *Concluding Unscientific Postscript*.

The fact that aesthetes express themselves in many different ways is quite beside the point, for inwardly and essentially they remain uncommitted as persons. They never undertake the task of living with an existential fear of the eternal. They avoid all paradox and suffering — or better, they *imagine* that they do — by making use of the expedient, *immediacy*.

---

[9] *Ibid.*, pp. 242-243. "Humor puts the eternal recollection of guilt together with everything, but does not by this recollection relate itself to an eternal happiness. Now we come to hidden inwardness. The eternal recollection of guilt cannot be expressed outwardly, it is incommensurable with such expression, since every outward expression finitizes guilt. But the eternal recollection of guilt which characterizes the hidden inwardness is anything but despair; for despair is always the infinite, the eternal, the total, at the instant of impatience; and all despair is a kind of bad temper. No, the eternal recollection is the mark indicative of the relationship to an eternal happiness, a mark which is as far as possible from being a plain indication, but which is always sufficient to prevent the leaping aside of despair. Humor discovers the comic by putting the total guilt together with the relativity as between man and man. The comic lies in the fact that the total guilt is the foundation which supports the whole comedy." *Ibid.*, pp. 492-493.

> *Immediacy is fortune,* for in the immediate consciousness there is no contradiction; the immediate individual is essentially seen as a fortunate individual, and *the view of life natural to immediacy* is one based on fortune. If one were to ask the immediate individual whence he has this view of life he would have to answer with virginal naïveté, "I do not myself understand it." The contradiction comes from without, and takes the form of misfortune. The immediate individual never comes to any understanding with misfortune, for he never becomes dialectical in himself; and if he does not manage to get rid of it, he finally reveals himself as lacking the poise to bear it.[10]

The aesthetic stage ranks lowest on the scale of responsible existence because it acknowledges no connection between degrees of personal being and degrees of personal involvement. The consistent aesthete just *is;* he never is *becoming.* And the tragedy is that he either doesn't see, or he doesn't want to see, that true existential being is only established by accepting the risk of becoming.

While Kierkegaard never for a moment looked with indifference on what we may call *obvious* examples of the aesthetic stage — namely, those whose goal in life is to have all the outward, sensual pleasure possible — he saved his profoundest remarks for examples which were *not* so obvious: those of philosophers and poets.

Philosophy tends to lead people astray (so Kierkegaard presumed) by encouraging them to think that the *rational* self is the *highest* self, and that the object of thought is the truly real. "In our age it is believed that knowledge settles everything, and that if a man only acquires a knowledge of the truth, the more briefly and the more quickly the better, he is helped. But to *exist* and to *know* are two very different things."[11] Kierkegaard had no personal objection to the act of thinking as such, just as long as *thinking* about reality was not used as a substitute for responsible existence. "To ask with infinite interest about a reality which is not one's own, is faith, and this constitutes a paradoxical relationship to the paradoxical. Aesthetically it is impossible to raise such a question except in thoughtlessness,

---

[10] *Ibid.,* p. 388.
[11] *Ibid.,* p. 264 (italics are mine).

since possibility is aesthetically higher than reality. . . . The aesthetic and intellectual principle is that no reality is thought or understood until its *esse* has been resolved into its *posse*."[12]

Even though Kierkegaard took this position, we must not conclude that he had any intrinsic objections to the art of philosophizing itself. He merely objected to philosophy's tendency to serve as a substitute for faith. Thus, as he surveyed the spiritual complacency which seemed to cover Copenhagen like a garment, he traced a good deal of this complacency to the fundamental error of supposing that *thinking* about Christianity was the same as *being* a Christian. This is why he shouted from the housetops (as it were) that unless a person is willing to venture far out, God is not able to take hold of him.

> Let us take up the matter fundamentally, yet with all brevity. The Saviour of the world, our Lord Jesus Christ, did not come to the world to bring a doctrine; He never lectured. . . . His teaching in fact was His life, His presence among men. If anyone desired to be His disciple, His way of going about it, as can be seen from the Gospel, was quite another way than the method of lecturing. He said to such a man something like this: "Adventure a decisive action, then we can begin." What does that mean? It means that one does not become a Christian by hearing something about Christ, by reading something, by thinking thereupon, or while Christ still lived upon earth, by seeing Him once in a while, or by going and gaping at Him the whole day. No, what is required is a *predicament (situation)*: adventure upon a decisive action, so that thou dost become heterogeneous with the life of this world, unable any longer to have thy life in it, dost find thyself in conflict with it — then thou wilt gradually be brought into such a tension that thou wilt be able to be observant of what I am here saying (says Christ).[13]

As Kierkegaard viewed things, it was harder *not* to be a Christian than it was to *be* one, for a person is *born* a Christian — at least in the dense Lutheran culture of which Kierkegaard was a part. And if birth did not clinch the issue, a trivial amount

---

[12] *Ibid.*, p. 288.
[13] Kierkegaard, *For Self-Examination and Judge For Yourselves!* p. 200. Princeton University Press, Princeton, 1944. Translated by Walter Lowrie. Although Kierkegaard certainly made a strong point here, he somewhat overstated himself. A more careful exegesis of the gospels would show that Christ *did* at times resort to the teaching of doctrine.

of aesthetic give-and-take would. "One's life is essentially homogeneous with worldliness and with this world, and so one hears perhaps a little about Christianity, one reads a little, thinks a little about Christianity, has once in a while a religious mood — and so one is a believer and a Christian."[14]

> But when they had done away with the notion of becoming a Christian by means of a decisive action capable of bringing about the predicament (situation) in which it is decided whether one will be a Christian or not, then (for the sake at least of doing something) they put in its stead the notion of thinking about Christianity, supposing they would become Christians in this way, and intending to advance subsequently beyond faith; for they did not stop at faith — and this is not to be wondered at, for they did not start out like Luther from exaggeration with respect to works and then attain faith, but they began as a matter of course with faith, which "naturally" every man has.[15]

Kierkegaard also insisted that the *poet* illustrates both the futility and the frustration of aestheticism — even though it seems that he made no effort to draw a careful distinction between the various schools of poets, a distinction which would have gone far in protecting Kierkegaard against the charge of oversimplification. "Reality is for the poet merely an occasion, a point of departure, from which he goes in search of the ideality of the possible."[16] When the poet addresses himself to religious issues, he adds pathos to pathos; for the religious stage must pass through the ethical stage, and poetry is too far in the clouds to deal with the concrete, existential terms of ethical living.

> For an existing individual the concept of an eternal happiness is essentially related to his mode of existence, and hence to the ideality of the actual; his pathos must be correspondingly qualified. If we conceive of love aesthetically, we must acknowledge the principle that the poet's ideal of love may be higher than anything that reality presents. The poet may possess an ideality in this connection such that what the actual life yields in comparison is but a feeble reflection. . . . The pathos of the poet is therefore essentially imaginative pathos. An attempt ethically

[14] *Ibid.*, p. 203.
[15] *Idem.*
[16] Kierkegaard, *Concluding Unscientific Postscript*, p. 347.

> to establish a poetic relationship to reality is therefore a misunderstanding, a backward step.... As for the religious, it is an essential requirement that it should have passed through the ethical. A religious poet is therefore in a peculiar position. Such a poet will seek to establish a relation to the religious through the imagination; but for this very reason he succeeds only in establishing an aesthetic relationship to something aesthetic.[17]

There is obviously an inconsequential difference between a philosophical and a poetic approach to the real — obvious, that is, when we confine ourselves to the terms of Kierkegaard's existential methodology — for both philosophy and poetry tend to classify *possibility* under the heading of *actuality*.

> A poetic temperament, which through the influence of circumstances, upbringing, and the like, has received a direction away from the theater to the Church, may therefore serve to bring about much confusion. Dazzled by the aesthetic in him, people believe that he is a religious personality, alas, even an *outstanding* personality, although perhaps he is not religious at all. Precisely this qualification of being *outstanding* is an aesthetic reminiscence, since from the religious point of view there is nothing validly outstanding, except an Apostle's paradoxical-dialectical authority. To be outstanding in the religious sphere constitutes precisely a step backward, by virtue of the qualitative dialectic which separates the different spheres from one another. The pathos of such an individual is poetic pathos, the pathos of the possible, with reality serving him as an occasion.[18]

The issue, it seems, is not quite the same as that expressed by Aristotle in his *Poetics*. While Aristotle acknowledged (1) that a poet might fail to make it clear that he was only speaking of either opinion or of what ought to be, or (2) that a poet might accidentally err while trying to tell what is, Kierkegaard charged that poetry was designed as a convenient substitute for the suffering which makes up the stuff of existential being. The world's great poets no doubt would wonder if such a charge has any validity.

As we continue our reading, we find that Kierkegaard was also a foe of the aesthetic stage because he was convinced that the

---

[17] *Ibid.*, pp. 347-348.
[18] *Ibid.*, p. 348.

aesthete, with his disturbing habit of taking neither time nor personal duty seriously, shuffled along under the illusion that wishing would make it so. Kierkegaard conceded that *some* things could properly be made the object of a wish; but there was *one* thing which could not, and that is eternal happiness.

> Aesthetically it is quite in order to wish for wealth, good fortune, and the most beautiful of damsels; in short, to wish for anything that is subject to an aesthetic dialectic. But *at the same time* to *wish* for an eternal happiness is doubly nonsense. Partly because it is *at the same time,* thus transforming an eternal happiness into something like a present on the Christmas tree; and partly because it is a *wish,* an eternal happiness being essentially relevant to an essentially existing individual, not related by an aesthetic dialectic to a romantically wishful individual. However, this concept must often enough content itself with being included among other bon-bons, and it is regarded as *tres bien* for one so to include it; indeed, this is often looked upon as the maximum of what may be asked for in this connection. And more than this, for with respect to the other goods in life, it is not exactly customary to suppose that they may be acquired merely by wishing for them; but an eternal happiness is supposed to come if one merely wishes for it. Experience teaches that the goods of fortune are unequally distributed, inequality being the dialectic to which the concept of fortune is subject. But an eternal happiness, which has been transformed in this manner into a gift of fortune, is nevertheless supposed to be distributed equally to all who wish for it. Here we have a double confusion. In the first place, the confusion that an eternal happiness is put on a level with an exceptionally fat living and the like; in the second place, the supposition that it is nevertheless distributed *equally,* which is a contradiction when applied to one of the gifts of fortune.[19]

The most effective means of escape from the pathos of the aesthetic stage is found in the cleansing despair which accompanies the melancholy of boredom. "There comes a moment in man's life when his immediacy is, as it were, ripened and the spirit demands a higher form in which it will apprehend itself as spirit."[20] Certainly nothing is more firmly established in the contemporary science of psychiatry than the fact that many

[19] *Ibid.,* p. 351.
[20] Kierkegaard, *Either/Or,* II, 159.

patients suffer from a feeling of emptiness and senselessness, rather than from some clinically classifiable neurosis. The inimitable sage, Samuel Johnson, brilliantly reviewed the illusion under which many restless aesthetes labor:

> The general remedy of those, who are uneasy without knowing the cause, is change of place; they are willing to imagine that their pain is the consequence of some local inconvenience, and endeavour to fly from it, as children from their shadows; always hoping for some more satisfactory delight from every new scene, and always returning home with disappointments and complaints. . . . It is common for a man, who feels pain, to fancy that he could bear it better in any other part . . . . He would, upon the trial, have been soon convinced, that the fountain of content must spring up in the mind: and that he who has so little knowledge of human nature, as to seek happiness by changing any thing but his own dispositions, will waste his life in fruitless efforts, and multiply the griefs which he purposes to remove.[21]

In boredom, of course, there emerges the possibility of either a forward or a backward movement. If the aroused spirit is properly directed, a transformation for the good may result. The hope of restored individuality becomes a live possibility. But if spirit is frustrated, this frustration will be communicated to the self in the form of melancholy.

> Man, so long as he is immediate spirit, coheres with the whole earthly life, and now the spirit would collect itself, as it were, out of this dispersion and become in itself transformed, the personality would be conscious of itself in its eternal validity. If this does not come to pass, if the movement is checked, if it is forced back, melancholy ensues. One may do much by way of inducing forgetfulness, one may work, one may employ other expedients more innocent than those of Nero, but melancholy remains. There is something inexplicable in melancholy.[22]

Although Kierkegaard labored hard to create a state of unrest in the heart of a complacent aesthete, he nonetheless realized that he could only go so far. True, existential decision has to arise from within the aesthete himself — with the help which comes from God, of course. If a follower of aesthetic interests

---

[21] Samuel Johnson, *The Rambler*, No. 6.
[22] Kierkegaard, *Either/Or*, II, 159.

reviews his fate, but determines to continue as he is, nothing more can be done.

C. *The Ethical Stage*

At this point let us recall Kierkegaard's emphatic insistence that man is a synthesis of the finite and the eternal. If the aesthete tends to view himself within the *finite,* the ethicist tends to view himself within the *eternal.* The ethicist hopes to reach authentic being by a realization of universal obligation. Spirit is taking the highest possible course as the self sustains a dedication to what it believes is an essential and profound manifestation of becoming. "Ethically, the individual subject is infinitely important. Take any human passion whatever, and let it come into contact with the ethical in the individual: this will ethically have great significance, historically perhaps none at all, perhaps again a great one; for the world-historical comes into being through what is ethically a perhaps."[23] A person enters the ethical stage the moment he perceives a serious relation between (1) the essence of the self, (2) the necessity of moment-by-moment choosing, and (3) a sense of duty which is nourished by the eternal. "He does not become another man than he was before, but he becomes himself, consciousness is unified, and he is himself."[24] In other words, a serious shift from indifference to responsibility takes place. "Ethically the ideality is the real within the individual himself. The real is an inwardness that is infinitely interested in existing; this is exemplified in the ethical individual."[25] The resulting involvement of the self with duty issues in a solemnity which a complacent aesthete can never experience. "What is the aesthetical in a man, and what is the ethical? To this I would reply: the aesthetical in a man is that by which he is immediately what he is; the ethical is that whereby he becomes what he becomes."[26]

The ethical stage is enveloped in an either/or atmosphere in which the self inwardly realizes for the first time that the very

[23] Kierkegaard, *Concluding Unscientific Postscript,* p. 132.
[24] Kierkegaard, *Either/Or,* II, 149.
[25] Kierkegaard, *Concluding Unscientific Postscript,* p. 289.
[26] Kierkegaard, *Either/Or,* II, 150.

being or non-being of the self is at stake. "The act of choosing is essentially a proper and stringent expression of the ethical. Whenever in a stricter sense there is question of an either/or, one can always be sure that the ethical is involved. The only absolute either/or is the choice between good and evil, but that is also absolutely ethical."[27]

Lest we make the mistake of classifying the ethical stage as some sort of abstraction, however, let us remember Kierkegaard's major thesis, "Truth is subjectivity." Since ethical truth pertains to the ethical state of the human subject, the *real* difference between good and evil is most clearly disclosed in conduct and not thought. "Think anything you will, think the most abstract of all categories, think the most concrete, you never think under the rubric of good and evil; think the whole of history, and you think the necessary movements of ideas, but you never think under the rubric of good and evil. You are constantly thinking relative differences, never the absolute difference."[28] This emphasis connects with Kierkegaard's view of man as a synthesis of the infinite and the finite, a synthesis which is only completed by existential, passionate *being*, never by comfortable, easily directed *thought*. Hence, the ethical "is quite difficult to realize — equally difficult for the wise and for the simple, since the difficulty does not lie in understanding it. If it were a matter of understanding, the clever would have a great advantage."[29] This is a very crucial point, indeed.

Once again, however, it seems that Kierkegaard's enthusiasm to elevate the importance of personal responsibility betrayed him into a kind of pragmatism which ended up downgrading the relevance of both universal and objective criteria in the application of ethics to daily life.

> If you will understand me aright, I should like to say that in making a choice it is not so much a question of choosing the right as of the energy, the earnestness, the pathos with which one chooses. Thereby the personality announces its inner infinity, and thereby, in turn, the personality is consolidated.

---

[27] *Ibid.*, p. 141.
[28] *Ibid.*, p. 188.
[29] Kierkegaard, *Concluding Unscientific Postscript*, p. 350.

Therefore, even if a man were to choose the wrong, he will nevertheless discover, precisely by reason of the energy with which he chose, that he had chosen wrong. For the choice being made with the whole inwardness of his personality, his nature is purified and he himself brought into immediate relation to the eternal Power whose omnipresence interpenetrates the whole of existence. This transfiguration, this higher consecration, is never attained by that man who chooses merely aesthetically.[30]

The ethical stage, let us remember, is no more able to serve as a resting place for spirit than is the aesthetic stage. Just as the awakened aesthete is seized by the terms of the ethical stage, so the awakened ethicist is seized by the terms of the religious stage. The ethical stage prepares the way for the religious stage by acquainting the self with that which gives every promise of being a way of salvation for the self. "When an individual abandons himself to lay hold of something great outside him, his enthusiasm is aesthetic; when he forsakes everything to save himself, his enthusiasm is ethical."[31] This seems harmless enough, but suddenly it fathers a frightening sense of non-being; for the self lacks the moral and volitional qualities needed to translate the absolute requirements of ethics into consistent daily action. If the self tries to flee from the absolute, it merely converts the threat of personal non-being into actuality. But if the self determines to mediate the absolute in time, it merely increases its feeling of guilt and frustration.

Legalists imagine that it is easy to develop such an interest in absolute goodness that the self can actually express the content of the eternal in time. "Now the comedy begins."[32] The comedy is traced to the contradiction which is bred by the predicament which accompanies "Synthesis B." Common people — those who have not been deceived into thinking that the self can complete its being by the development of an absolute ethical interest — look upon a legalist with a sense of wonder because of the way he makes this world seem irrelevant through his other-worldly dedication. "The judgment of men upon such an individual will always be: for him there is nothing that is im-

---

[30] Kierkegaard, *Either/Or*, II, 141.
[31] Kierkegaard, *Concluding Unscientific Postscript*, p. 350.
[32] *Ibid.*, p. 451.

portant. And why not? Because for him the ethical is absolutely important, differing in this from men in general, for whom so many things are important, aye, nearly everything, but nothing absolutely important."[33] As long as the ethicist persists in using irony as an incognito, he will be no more successful in mediating the eternal in time than the aesthete is.

A spiritually honest person will forthrightly acknowledge that the self has failed to close the gap between what it *is* and what it *ought to be*. The resulting feeling of self-despair will then serve as a valuable guide to the religious stage. Existentially understood, therefore, the absolute nature of ethics is a means by which the self, confronted with despair, finds its way to a life of faith and hope.

> Ethics is after all an ideal science, and that not only in the sense that every other science is ideal. Ethics bring [sic] ideality into reality; on the other hand its movement is not designed to raise reality up into ideality. Ethics points to ideality as a task and assumes that man is in possession of the conditions requisite for performing it. Thereby ethics develops a contradiction, precisely for the fact that it makes the difficulty and the impossibility clear.[34]

An existential mediation of the eternal in time is a literal impossibility; but when a legalist is reminded that he is defending an approach to life which inevitably draws man into the center of a painful contradiction, he just snivels. He doesn't dare concede the possibility that faith and hope rank higher than the total surrender of the self to an absolute ethical interest.

"The more ideal ethics is, the better. It must not let itself be disturbed by the twaddle that it is no use requiring the impossible; for even to listen to such talk is unethical, is something for which ethics has neither *time* nor *opportunity*."[35]

---

[33] *Idem*.
[34] Kierkegaard, *The Concept of Dread*, p. 15.
[35] *Idem*. "The enthusiastic ethicist therefore will not resent the objections or the ridicule; long before this befalls him he will have realized that it would befall him, he will be as ready as the best of them to construe his effort as comic — and then with calm resolve he will choose to use the understanding to see what the shrewdest thing is . . . in order not to do it. [For] . . . in him there is no breach, nor the suffering involved in the breach." Kierkegaard, *Concluding Unscientific Postscript*, pp. 504-505.

Authentic existence finds its outlet in the instant, an atom of eternity; and this takes place either by a direct fulfilment of the absolute terms of ethics, which is a living impossibility; or by an exercise of faith, which is the tried and tested way of a true Christian.

Since the struggles of man in both the aesthetic and ethical stages have led to nothing but pathos, self-sufficiency has been effectively challenged.

D. *The Religious Stage*

Now that we are about to examine the highest expression of the dialectic of inwardness, it is important to remember that the stages not only overlap but also nourish one another. Hence, we would do Kierkegaard a grave injustice, were we to imply that the stages, though collectively forming the anatomy of daily living, are absolutely separate and unique. Lowrie makes this clear in his introduction to the *Concluding Unscientific Postscript*: "For the word 'stage' seems to imply that with each advance the preceding stage is definitely left behind. But even in the *Stages,* Climacus spoke more commonly of the 'spheres' of existence, and it is evident that the spheres overlap and penetrate one another."[36] It seems that each stage sanctifies and completes all that is relevant in the stage or stages leading up to it.

In turning to the religious stage, however, we confront what seems to be a series of boxes one within another; or at least we confront a troublesome number of subdivisions, a characteristic not found in either the aesthetic or the ethical stage.

But perhaps we should not be too surprised by this complexity, for after all Kierkegaard developed his methodology as an expedient to help goad others into a position where they would accept the Christian faith with the seriousness which it deserves.

Furthermore, Kierkegaard was more concerned to show *how* to become a Christian, rather than engage in an erudite exercise by showing *what* Christianity is.

---

[36] Pages xix-xx.

The decision lies in the subject. The appropriation is the paradoxical inwardness which is specifically different from all other inwardness. The thing of being a Christian is not determined by the *what* of Christianity but by the *how* of the Christian. This *how* can only correspond with one thing, the absolute paradox . . . . precisely because people in our age and in the Christendom of our time do not appear to be sufficiently aware of the dialectic of inward appropriation, or of the fact that the "how" of the individual is an expression just as precise and more decisive for what he has, than is the "what" to which he appeals . . . .[37]

The *how* is actually another reference to the judgment, "Truth is subjectivity," just as the *what* is another reference to the concept of objectivity. As Kierkegaard took inventory of the church in Copenhagen, he decided that it was very easy to know *what* Christianity is, while it was frightening to know *how* to become a Christian. And since Kierkegaard was revolted by what he believed were caricatures of religious truth, he vowed to deal with what was frightening, both to himself and to others. Reality (the ethical) is within the self, and no person has the least right to call himself a Christian until he has endured a great deal of suffering in the inner man.

Existential suffering, which is the most authentic sign of the religious stage, forms a carefully conceived and executed *telos* in Kierkegaard's writing. "Becoming a Christian is then the most fearful decision of a man's life, a struggle through to attain faith against despair and offense, the twin Cerberuses that guard the entrance to a Christian life."[38]

By way of transition, however, let us note the inner disgust which Kierkegaard felt when he contemplated the way philosophers and theologians formulated rational "proofs" of God's existence. This kind of logical exercise brought no inner suffering; rather, it brought a conceited sense of intellectual triumph, and this conceit was further evidence that both philosophers

---

[37] Kierkegaard, *Concluding Unscientific Postscript*, pp. 540-541. "The possibility of knowing what Christianity is without being a Christian must therefore be affirmed." *Ibid.*, p. 332.
[38] *Ibid.*, p. 333.

The Dialectic of Inwardness

and theologians tended to fear the want of prestige more than they feared the person of God.

> So rather let us sin, sin out and out, seduce maidens, murder men, commit highway robbery — after all, that can be repented of, and such a criminal God can still get a hold on. But this proud superiority which has risen to such a height scarcely can be repented of, it has a semblance of profundity which it deserves. So rather let us mock God, out and out, as has been done before in the world — this is always preferable to the disparaging air of importance with which one would prove God's existence. For to prove the existence of one who is present is the most shameless affront, since it is an attempt to make him ridiculous; but unfortunately people have no inkling of this and for sheer seriousness regard it as a pious undertaking. But how could it occur to anybody to prove that he exists, unless one had permitted oneself to ignore him, and now makes the thing all the worse by proving his existence before his very nose?[39]

Whether this argument is valid or not is a separate question, but certainly, apart from a few outbursts in the *Journals,* it would be very difficult to find a more cutting passage in all the writings of Kierkegaard.

This passage is backed up by a conviction which is repeated *ad nauseam,* namely, that only passionately embraced paradox, never objective thinking, is the means by which a person mediates the eternal in time, thus completing "Synthesis B." ". . . one should not think slightly of the paradoxical; for the paradox is the source of the thinker's passion, and the thinker without paradox is like a lover without feeling: a paltry mediocrity."[40] Since philosophical and theological proofs for God try to eliminate the paradox, it follows, says Kierkegaard, that the connection between offense and Christianity is threatened. "In the last resort, the occasion of offense applies to an individual who is in relationship to the essential when one would make new to him that which he essentially believes he possesses. He who has no religiousness at all cannot possibly be offended at Christianity, and the reason why the possibility of offense lay so close to the Jews was that they stood closest to Christianity.

---

[39] *Ibid.,* p. 485.
[40] Kierkegaard, *Philosophical Fragments,* p. 29.

If Christianity had wanted merely to add something new to the old, it could have aroused offense only relatively; but precisely because it wanted to take all the old and make it new, the offense lay so close to it."[41] Existentially and inwardly there is a *right* way to prove the divine presence, "for one proves his presence by an expression of submission, which may assume various forms according to the customs of the country — and thus it is also one proves God's existence by worship . . . not by proofs."[42]

Submission to paradox will remain offensive to those who relativize Christianity by giving an advantage to people who, by fortune, happen to have a high intelligence quotient. When Kierkegaard explained what it means to be "crucified with Christ," therefore, he insisted upon the crucifixion of any and all advantages — especially that of the intellect. He presumed that this would go a long way in rendering every human being essentially related to the absolute.[43]

> . . . if it is a pitiable error to want to be like God by reason of virtue and holiness, instead of becoming more and more humble, it is more ludicrous to want to be that in consideration of having an exceptionally clever mind; for virtue and holiness do after all stand in an essential relation to God's nature, and the other determinant makes God Himself ridiculous as the *tertium comparationis*. He who in truth has given up his understanding and believes against the understanding (which is like rolling a burden up a mountain), such a man will be prevented from playing the genius on the score of his religiousness.[44]

This matter is easier to state than to realize, however, for precisely what steps do we take in order that we may find our way into the religious stage?

At this point Kierkegaard would very probably advise us to meditate once again upon the concept of dread, for dread, which we may usefully speak of as "anxiety," forms a vital part of the self in its existential suffering. In fact, dread locates one form of offense within the living self. The self longs to be free; but

---

[41] Kierkegaard, *Concluding Unscientific Postscript*, p. 480n.
[42] *Ibid.*, p. 485. Rational, objective proofs, that is.
[43] It is safe to say that this argument promises more than it delivers, for not all people are equally capable of crucifying the understanding.
[44] Kierkegaard, *Concluding Unscientific Postscript*, pp. 501-502.

then it is often seized by anxiety when it confronts the simultaneous responsibilities and impossibilities which emerge as spirit soars in freedom. The self refuses to surrender its freedom, of course, and yet it experiences new dread whenever the moral ideal contained in freedom is acknowledged by the inner self. In fact, the self is shocked to discover that the very *being* of the self stands or falls according to the earnestness with which the self is ethical. Such a shock is really a covert form of the fear of death, for the threat of non-being which follows an immoral act is remarkably similar to the threat of non-being posed by death itself. In other words, the loss of dignity and self-respect *is* a kind of death.

In the case of people whose spirits have never soared in moral freedom, dread is only a potency. Such people are spared the suffering of personal freedom because they are in a state of spiritual dreaming. Dreaming spirits — as found in children — would rather ride freedom to the mysterious and the adventurous, than increase their perception of the conflict between desire and fulfilment, a conflict which makes up the very stuff of finitude. If dreaming continues and continues, long after maturity has been given a chance to express itself, we are dealing with spiritual sickness, and the general methodology of Kierkegaard is rendered irrelevant. Unless the dialectic of inwardness is active, it is meaningless to speak about existence-spheres.

As soon as a person normally matures, however, he inevitably becomes an illustration of Kierkegaard's thesis that *man* is the locus of both paradox and personal guilt.

> The qualitative leap is outside of ambiguity, but he who through dread becomes guilty is innocent, for it was not he himself but dread, an alien power which laid hold of him, a power which he loved and yet dreaded — and yet he is guilty, he who after all loved it while he feared it.[45]

Thus a married man may find himself casting erotic glances at an attractive maiden. He enjoys the fantasied lust, while at the same time he feels ashamed of himself. Or again, a man may find temporary release through alcohol, though he is dis-

---

[45] Kierkegaard, *The Concept of Dread*, p. 39.

gusted by the resulting bondage. In any event, Kierkegaard was convinced that the experience of simultaneous attraction and revulsion was no reason for questioning the guilt of the participating self.

Functionally and existentially, therefore, man is innocent as long as spirit remains dormant. But innocence vanishes, and the self tastes one species of guilt or another, the moment spirit is aroused. Since freedom often creates a state of ambivalence in the affections, the awakened self ends up loving what it hates. Herein is the paradox.

Guilt forms an essential ingredient in the religious stage because it is the most concrete expression of existence thus far discussed. Abstraction seeks to nullify the seriousness of guilt by comforting the self with concepts which supposedly originate *sub specie aeternitatis*.

When we contemplate the significance of guilt, however, we must remember that the question of *quantity* is irrelevant; for the first offense — the primal loss of innocence through the experience of dread — is sufficient to create an eternal yoke if it is seen in relation to the eternal. "For human justice pronounces a life sentence only for the third offense, but eternity pronounces sentence the first time forever. He is caught forever, harnessed with the yoke of guilt, and never gets out of the harness. . . ."[46]

Although the admission of guilt is crucial in the religious stage, Kierkegaard insisted that it was necessary to go on to the admission of *essential* guilt. Essential guilt is but another name for total guilt. All expressions of childish or relative guilt are impotent to play a decisive role in the religious stage, for unless an existing individual comes to terms with essential guilt, he will refuse to take a deep plunge into authentic existence; that is, he will refuse to contemplate the meaning of life in its relation to eternal happiness.

> The priority of the total guilt is not to be determined empirically, is no *summa summarum;* for no determination of totality ever results from numerical computation. The totality of guilt comes into being for the individual when he puts his guilt together with the relation to an eternal happiness. Hence we began as

[46] Kierkegaard, *Concluding Unscientific Postscript*, p. 475.

> we did by affirming that the consciousness of guilt is the decisive expression for the relationship to an eternal happiness. He who has no relation to this never gets to the point of conceiving himself as totally or essentially guilty. The very least guilt — even if from that time on the individual were an angel — when it is put together with a relationship to an eternal happiness, is enough, for the composition determines the quality.⁴⁷

Kierkegaard painstakingly cites examples of "lower" guilt, but only to show that "every conception of guilt is lower which does not by an eternal recollection put guilt together with the relation to an eternal happiness, but by memory puts it together with something lower, something comparative (one's own fortuitous situation or that of another man), and allows forgetfulness to step between the particular instances of guilt."⁴⁸

It may seem that we have exhausted the heights of the religious stage by our reference to essential guilt. Not so — and this may help us appreciate the reason why Kierkegaard drew such a sharp line between guilt and sin. Once more, and by no means for the last time, the shadow of immanence falls upon the self to limit and corrupt.

> That is to say, the consciousness of guilt still lies essentially in immanence, in distinction from the consciousness of sin. In the consciousness of guilt it is the selfsame subject which becomes essentially guilty by keeping guilt in relationship to an eternal happiness, but yet the identity of the subject is such that guilt does not make the subject a new man, which is the characteristic of the breach. But the breach, in which lies the paradoxical accentuation, cannot occur in the relationship between an exister and the eternal, because the eternal embraces the exister on all sides, and therefore the disrelationship or incompatibility remains within immanence.⁴⁹

The crux of the issue seems to be this: that the factor of guilt, even though it is related to eternal happiness, can be managed in such a way that it is not a *decisive* expression of existential, passionate selfhood. In other words, Kierkegaard had a suspicion that the self, though fraught with guilt, could escape from

---

⁴⁷ *Ibid.*, pp. 471-472.
⁴⁸ *Ibid.*, pp. 480-481.
⁴⁹ *Ibid.*, p. 474.

the responsibility of seeing itself in relation to God, the absolute.

Once again Kierkegaard turned to the concept of dread; only this time he shrewdly went beyond the moral ambivalence which the self often suffers when, through a soaring of spirit, the self finds that it simultaneously loves and hates something. A more dreadful view of dread — one which exposes evil with a force closely approaching demonstration — is man's dread of the *good*. This species of dread, according to Kierkegaard, is closely connected with the demoniacal in human nature.

> . . . I must reply that the demoniacal is a state. Out of this state the particular sinful act can break forth perpetually. But the state is a possibility, although again in relation to freedom it is a reality posited by the qualitative leap. The demoniacal is dread of the good. In the state of innocence freedom was not posited as freedom, its possibility appears in the dread of the individuality. In the demoniacal the situation is reversed. Freedom is posited as unfreedom, for freedom is lost. The possibility of freedom is in turn dread. The difference is absolute; for the possibility of freedom manifests itself here in relation to unfreedom, which is exactly the opposite of innocence, which is a determinant oriented towards freedom.[50]

It would be well, at this point, to recall that the pith and marrow of ethical duty is love. Now we are confronted with the fact that the very prospect of having to meet the terms of love often issues in a dread of the good. This constitutes Kierkegaard's primary proof that man is a sinner. Since true love calls for a non-judgmental sharing of life with life, self-centeredness shrinks from the responsibility of carrying out the terms of love. Intellectual assent can easily be given to the ethic of love, of course, but this is not the same as *living* a life of love.

Only ethical and ethical-religious elements are essentially related to the self which is awakened into a state of sin by spirit's flight through freedom; and these elements are essential because they serve as means by which the self is closed up to the exhausting task of mediating the eternal in time. "The self is the conscious synthesis of infinitude and finitude which re-

---

[50] Kierkegaard, *The Concept of Dread,* p. 109.

lates itself to itself, whose task is to become itself, a task which can be performed only by means of a relationship to God."[51]

It is ironic that despair sires hope. Still, the fact remains that a person will not see the necessity of giving an absolute place to the absolute until he despairs of all that is connected with finitude.

When Kierkegaard turned to the specific task of defining sin, he not only avoided the objective tone found in many classical catechisms, but he determined to connect his definition with the following two existential concepts: (1) that finitude issues in moral and ethical despair, and (2) that "Truth is subjectivity." "Sin is this: *before God, or with the conception of God, to be in despair at not willing to be oneself, or in despair at willing to be oneself.*"[52] The first despair normally accompanies flagrant transgressions of the law, while the second normally accompanies the more subtle pretences of self-righteousness.

Our sickness as sinners, let us note, is *unto death*. All sorts of palliatives may be tried, but the sickness remains. Therefore, it is a sign of personal ignorance to assume that the critical difference between a Christian and a pagan is decided by the criterion of sickness, for both are sick. The critical difference is that the Christian *acknowledges* his sickness, whereas the pagan desperately clings to the optimism that all is well.

The pagan may pass through the valley and shadow of melancholy, but he sees no connection between this experience and personal sin. Kierkegaard sharply disagrees.

> There is something inexplicable in melancholy. The man who has sorrow and anxiety knows why he is sorrowful or anxious. If a melancholy man is asked what grounds he has for it, what it is that weighs upon him, he will reply, "I know not, I cannot explain it." Herein lies the infinity of melancholy. This reply is perfectly correct, for as soon as a man knows the cause, the melancholy is done away with, whereas, on the contrary, in the case of the sorrowful the sorrow is not done away when a man knows why he sorrows. But melancholy is sin, really it is

[51] Kierkegaard, *The Sickness Unto Death*, p. 44.
[52] *Ibid.*, p. 123.

a sin *instar omnium*, for not to will deeply and sincerely is sin, and this is the mother of all sins.⁵³

Since the two words, *before God*, comprise the most important part of Kierkegaard's definition of sin, at least three complementary inferences can be introduced at this point.

First, sin is located in a defiant will, rather than in an intellect which, by dint of circumstances, is either inconsistent in its judgments or just plain indolent. This provides Kierkegaard with another convenient opportunity to explain the reason for his break with Socrates.

> What determinant is it then that Socrates lacks in determining what sin is? It is will, defiant will. The Greek intellectualism was too happy, too naïve, too aesthetic, too ironical, too witty ... to be able to get it sinfully into its head that a person knowingly could fail to do the good, or knowingly, with knowledge of what was right, do what was wrong. The Greek spirit proposes an intellectual categorical imperative.⁵⁴

Second, sin is an existence-determinant. "... sin is not a state. Its idea is that its concept is constantly annulled. As a state (*de potentia*) it *is* not, whereas *de actu* or *in actu* it is and is again."⁵⁵ This means that sin is neither a doctrine nor an object of thought. It penetrates the conscious self whenever the self responsibly and passionately acknowledges that a serious gap exists between the self as it is and the self as it ought to be.

Third, the possibility of sin increases the possibility of intellectual offense. And precisely *where* does this possibility of offense lie? "It lies in the fact that a man, as a particular individual, should have such a reality as is implied by existing directly in the sight of God; and then again, and as a consequence of this, that a man's sin should concern God."⁵⁶

---

⁵³ *Either/Or*, II, 159-160. This, indeed, is a strange quotation. Kierkegaard must be using the terms "melancholy" and "anxiety" in very restricted senses, for contemporary psychiatry has shown again and again that many patients suffering from anxiety are no more able to give a reason for their suffering than those who are troubled by melancholy — now referred to as "depression."
⁵⁴ Kierkegaard, *The Sickness Unto Death*, p. 145.
⁵⁵ Kierkegaard, *The Concept of Dread*, p. 14.
⁵⁶ Kierkegaard, *The Sickness Unto Death*, p. 133.

The Dialectic of Inwardness

Since man's sickness is unto death, and since man does not actuate his true essence until he existentially mediates the eternal in time, Kierkegaard's stress on sin as an existence-determinant before God goes far in fortifying the claim that man's experience of despair is anchored in his *essential* failure to live with singleness of mind toward that which is absolute. Relief from despair comes only when the self is so governed by eternity that a radical transformation of the self results.

> That which really makes a man despair is not misfortune, but it is the fact that he lacks the eternal; despair is to lack the eternal; despair consists in not having undergone the change of eternity by duty's "shalt." Consequently despair is not the loss of the beloved, that is misfortune, pain, suffering; but despair is the lack of the eternal.[57]

From this it would seem probable that Kierkegaard has gone just about as far as he can in detailing the religious stage. More careful investigation shows, however, that this is not quite the case, for an expression of existence called "religiousness A" stands between the experience of despair and the paradoxical religion which Kierkegaard defends as true Christianity, existentially interpreted.

But the nature of religiousness A is so extremely difficult to comprehend, that in fairness to Kierkegaard we shall quote his exact words. As we reflect on these words, however, let us remember that Kierkegaard dedicated himself to the unique and strange goal of making it difficult to become a Christian. He realized that "Religiousness A can exist in paganism, and in Christianity it can be the religiousness of everyone who is not decisively Christian, whether he be baptized or no."[58] A person in religiousness A is not far from the kingdom, to be sure, but he is just far enough to fall short of true Christianity. "The distinction between the pathetic and the dialectical must, however, be more closely defined; for religiousness A is by no means undialectic, but it is not paradoxically dialectic. Religiousness A is the dialectic of inward transformation; it is the relation to

---

[57] Kierkegaard, *Works of Love*, p. 34.
[58] Kierkegaard, *Concluding Unscientific Postscript*, p. 495.

an eternal happiness which is not conditioned by anything but is the dialectic inward appropriation of the relationship, and so is conditioned only by the inwardness of the appropriation and its dialectic."[59]

Kierkegaard continues: "In religiousness A an eternal happiness is something simple, and the pathetic becomes the dialectical factor in the dialectic of inward-appropriation. . . ."[60] Again, "Religiousness A makes the thing of existing as strenuous as possible (outside the paradox-religious sphere), but it does not base the relation to an eternal happiness upon one's existence but lets the relation to an eternal happiness serve as basis for the transformation of existence. From the individual's relation to the eternal, there results the how of his existence, not the converse, and thereby infinitely more comes out of it than was put into it."[61] Socrates gazing into space, a subject of inner suffering, yet never for a moment surrendering the confidence that he could devise some sort of an account of the self's relation to the eternal — this seems to give a satisfactory illustration of what is meant by religiousness A. Socrates sincerely sought to mediate the eternal in time, but he always had a ready word of rational self-defense.

The defective element in religiousness A, therefore, is that it does not go far enough. Lowrie nicely summarized the issue as follows:

> By religion A he [Kierkegaard] indicates the religiousness which is simply a heartfelt expression of a sense of God, or of the numinous, or of an expectation of an eternal blessedness, which is not conditioned by a definite something, but is merely heartfelt feeling itself, though in a sense it may be "dialectical". S. K. recognized that such religiousness may perfectly well exist in paganism. In fact this is precisely the quality of most of the religions of the world; and the great majority of those who are baptized and confirmed in the Church know no other sort. This is not to be taken as disparagement of religion A, which in its loftiest exemplifications may well be regarded as man's tip-toe reach, the most exalted attainment of humanity. S. K. recognizes

---

[59] *Ibid.*, p. 494.
[60] *Ibid.*, p. 497.
[61] *Ibid.*, p. 509.

that 'religion A must be present in the individual before there can be any question of his becoming aware' of religion B . . . .[62]

But how does one bring himself to the place where he succeeds in going beyond religiousness A? This becomes a pressing question, indeed.

A question of this nature might upset others, but Kierkegaard actually gave the impression that he was delighted to handle it; and the reason for his enthusiasm is by no means difficult to explain. Since Kierkegaard realized that his literary efforts would fail to cause a stir unless he succeeded in finding some reason why it was equally difficult for men everywhere to become individuals and Christians (the same thing), it is only natural that he rejoiced when the right pathway seemed to open up before him. The route which he chose proved to be an offense to many, but the more offended they became the more certain he became that he was moving in the right direction.

Kierkegaard found precisely what he wanted in the biblical account of the incarnation. By interpreting the incarnation as the "absolute paradox" he felt he could establish (1) the uniqueness of Christianity, (2) the necessity of a "leap" of faith, and (3) the want of any advantage in being rationally clever. These three inferences go far in making up the essence of "religiousness B," the profoundest part of the religious stage.

God became man: this is the absolute paradox. Such an awesome event simply could not happen; and yet what could *not* happen *did* happen. Thus, the uniqueness of Christianity turns on what was neither anticipated before it took place, nor understood after it did. The incarnation is a shattering mystery; it is the paradox of paradoxes.

> The paradox consists principally in the fact that God, the Eternal, came into existence in time as a particular man. Whether this particular man is a servant or an emperor is neither here nor there, it is no more adequate for God to be king than to be a beggar; it is not a greater humiliation for God to become a beggar than to become an emperor . . . . If the childish orthodoxy insists on this humiliation as the paradox,

[62] Lowrie, *Kierkegaard*, p. 323.

> it shows *eo ipso* that it is not aware of the paradox .... If one would talk about God, let him say, God. That is the quality.[63]

It is not surprising, therefore, that Kierkegaard became quite disturbed when apologists tried to establish the uniqueness of Christianity by an appeal to the amazing fact that "Christ came into the world in order to suffer."[64] Kierkegaard acknowledged that suffering is one of the essential elements in the religious stage, and he also acknowledged that the world is full of suffering. But he refused to surrender the primacy of the absolute paradox. He contended that only a "childish orthodoxy" would either (a) base the uniqueness of Christianity upon Christ's suffering as Messiah, or (b) make suffering the *telos* of Christ's coming to earth.[65]

Now that we have reached the place where authentic faith is not expressed until the self passionately and existentially believes against the understanding by confronting the absolute paradox, little more remains to be said about the dialectic of inwardness. A review of the existence-spheres, however, may help us appreciate the relation between the aesthetic, ethical, and religious expressions of personal commitment.

> If the individual is in himself undialectical and has his dialectic outside himself, then we have the *aesthetic interpretation*. If the individual is dialectical in himself inwardly in self-assertion, hence in such a way that the ultimate basis is not dialectic in itself, inasmuch as the self which is at the basis is used to overcome and assert itself, then we have the *ethical interpretation*. If the individual is inwardly defined by self-annihilation before God, then we have *religiousness A*. If the individual is paradoxically dialectic, every vestige of original immanence being

---

[63] Kierkegaard, *Concluding Unscientific Postscript*, p. 528.
[64] *Ibid.*, p. 529.
[65] The methodology behind this rebuttal illustrates the little use that Kierkegaard made of the whole counsel of God in his more philosophical writings. I think it is not unfair to say that Christ *did* come into the world in order to bear the sins of the world through personal suffering. We must not conclude, however, that Kierkegaard emphasized the incarnation to the place where the atonement no longer had significance. "The only one who innocently sorrowed over sinfulness was Christ, but He who did not sorrow over it as a destiny which He must put up with, but He sorrowed as one who freely chose to bear all the sin of the world and to suffer its punishment." Kierkegaard, *The Concept of Dread*, p. 35.

annihilated and all connection cut off, the individual being brought to the utmost verge of existence, then we have *paradoxical religiousness* [religiousness B]. This paradoxical inwardness is the greatest possible, for even the most paradoxical determinant, if after all it is within immanence, leaves as it were a possibility of escape, of a leaping away, of a retreat into the eternal behind it; it is as though everything had not been staked after all. But the breach makes the inwardness the greatest possible.[66]

Fortunately Kierkegaard went on to compose a *second* review of the existence-spheres, only this time he used the very concept of existence itself as his criterion of judgment.

> *Immediacy, the aesthetic,* finds no contradiction in the fact of existing: to exist is one thing, and the contradiction is something else which comes from without. *The ethical* finds the contradiction, but within self-assertion. *The religiousness A* comprehends the contradiction as suffering in self-annihilation, although within immanence, but by ethically accentuating the fact of existing it prevents the exister from becoming abstract in immanence, or from becoming abstract by wishing to remain in immanence. *The paradoxical religiousness* breaks with immanence and makes the fact of existing the absolute contradiction, not within immanence, but against immanence. There is no longer any immanent fundamental kinship between the temporal and the eternal, because the eternal itself has entered time and would constitute there the kinship.[67]

Much of this will remain incomprehensible unless we remember Kierkegaard's unwavering conviction that a person will never know the meaning of true Christianity until he agrees, once and for all, to surrender the understanding as a ground of religious confidence. God became a man; this is an impossibility, judged by human understanding, and yet it happened. ". . . that which in accordance with its nature is eternal comes into existence in time, is born, grows up, and dies — this is a breach with all thinking."[68]

Does this place the self in a hopeless predicament? *By no means!* thundered Kierkegaard; for apart from a total break

---
[66] Kierkegaard, *Concluding Unscientific Postscript*, p. 507.
[67] *Ibid.*, pp. 507-508.
[68] *Ibid.*, p. 513.

with immanence, faith remains nothing but a potency. Confront the self with the absolute paradox, and the possibility of faith being expressed is greatly enhanced. An awakened self excitedly leaps into the mysteries of the eternal.

Such a leap implicates the self in an unavoidable risk, to be sure. The risk is unavoidable, contended Kierkegaard, because the totality of objective evidences for the Christian religion cannot rise above rational probability. But such probability, no matter how it is sliced and served up, is insufficient for faith.

Although Kierkegaard made little or no effort to defend his position at this point, he forthrightly assumed that existential commitment to God and complete subjective certainty are correlatives. Thus, a cheerful submission to objective risk is spiritual proof that the self has at last learned to live by faith, rather than by understanding. "For without risk there is no faith, and the greater the risk the greater the faith; the more objective security the less inwardness (for inwardness is precisely subjectivity), and the less objective security the more profound the possible inwardness."[69]

Many apologists and theologians would resist the notion that a vital connection exists between subjective faith and objective absurdity, but not Kierkegaard. Quite to the contrary, "Faith is the objective uncertainty due to the repulsion of the absurd held fast by the passion of inwardness, which in this instance is intensified to the utmost degree."[70] "What now is the absurd? The absurd is — that the eternal truth has come into being in time, that God has come into being, has been born, has grown up, and so forth, precisely like any other individual human being, quite indistinguishable from other individuals."[71]

We shall miss the point, however, unless we bear in mind that faith, which is the converse of sin, is an *existential determinant,* and thus communicates a spiritual quality to both the will and the affections which makes it possible for the self to mediate the eternal in time.

[69] *Ibid.,* p. 188.
[70] *Ibid.,* p. 540.
[71] *Ibid.,* p. 188.

Let us now call the untruth of the individual *Sin*. Viewed eternally he cannot be sin, nor can he be eternally presupposed as having been in sin. By coming into existence therefore (for the beginning was that subjectivity is untruth), he becomes a sinner. He is not born as a sinner in the sense that he is presupposed as being a sinner before he is born, but he is born in sin and as a sinner.[72]

This helps account for the rather cryptic expression used by Kierkegaard (and also by Reinhold Niebuhr) that "sin posits itself." The individual is not a sinner as long as spirit is dormant; nor would spirit, when aroused, betray the individual into sin unless the individual were already a sinner through unbelief.

The only truth which should passionately concern a Christian is this: whether the Christian *himself* is truth as a living subject. Subjective truth is *"an objective uncertainty held fast in an appropriation-process of the most passionate inwardness. . . ."*[73] Faith, it seems, brings subjective truth into being by the dedicated, spiritual manner in which it disengages the self from (a) all objective attempts to spell out an immanental sense of fulfilment and righteousness for the self, especially through the aid of the understanding; and from (b) all objective strategies which are designed to relieve the self of risk, suffering, and sin.

> Faith is precisely the contradiction between the infinite passion of the individual's inwardness and the objective uncertainty. If I am capable of grasping God objectively, I do not believe, but precisely because I cannot do this I must believe. If I wish to preserve myself in faith I must constantly be intent upon holding fast the objective uncertainty, so as to remain out upon the deep, over seventy thousand fathoms of water, still preserving my faith.[74]

Although Kierkegaard made no convincing effort to explain precisely how all of this takes place, it is enough if we emphasize the satisfaction he felt when he reached what he believed was the highest expression of the religious stage.

Before we terminate our efforts to explore the dialectic of in-

---

[72] *Ibid.*, p. 186.
[73] *Ibid.*, p. 182.
[74] *Idem.*

wardness, however, let us remember that Kierkegaard was sincerely convinced that he had succeeded in developing a concept of faith which equalized the risk which must be taken by every Christian. As he saw the matter, it makes no difference whether a person was a member of the first generation and happened to enjoy the privilege of talking with Christ directly, or whether by an act of faith he now confronts the absolute paradox as truth.[75] The state of inwardness is precisely the same in both cases.

> . . . a contemporary would constantly be reminded that he did not see or hear God immediately, but merely a humble human being who said of himself that he was God; in other words, he would constantly be reminded that the fact in question was based upon a self-contradiction. Would this man gain anything by reason of the reliability of his account? Historically speaking yes, but otherwise not. . . .[76]

The religious stage, though weakened by its emphasis on the absurd, is a *magnificent* attempt to make it fearfully plain that God is absolute; and that when we speak of God, we should mean *God*. The total self should be totally committed. A professing Christian is nothing but a plain fraud unless his daily life is transformed by the eternal. Let him suffer, and let him die; but never let him blaspheme the name of God by following such finite and relative standards that contingency becomes king. "For the religious always has to deal with total determinants, not learnedly (so that it looks away from the particular individual), but existentially, and hence it has to do with bringing the individual, by fair means or foul, directly or indirectly, in and under the totality, not in such a way as to disappear in it, but in such a way as to put him together with it."[77]

The present consolation of living within the requirements of total determinants is that suffering enriches the subjectivity of truth. And what could be more important than this, since

---

[75] This is not quite accurate. Certainly the disciples who witnessed the transfiguration of Christ enjoyed an advantage not shared by others.
[76] Kierkegaard, *Philosophical Fragments*, p. 77.
[77] Kierkegaard, *Concluding Unscientific Postscript*, pp. 478-479.

we are soon to die and face the judgment of God? ". . . for he who with quiet introspection is honest before God and concerned for himself, the Deity saves from being in error, though he be never so simple, him the Deity leads by the suffering of inwardness to the truth."[78]

[78] *Ibid.*, pp. 543-544.

Chapter Five

KINGDOM OUTCASTS

ALTHOUGH KIERKEGAARD SPENT HIS WHOLE LIFE DEFENDING the pivotal thesis, "Truth is subjectivity," it is quite inaccurate to suppose that all his energies were expended on the affirmative task of explaining why he believed this pivotal thesis was *pivotal*. As a shrewd Christian apologist he also attempted to refute the main positions which sought to eliminate the subjective character of truth. Three such positions occupied his attention: speculation, Hegelianism, and objectivity. At least these are the three which stand out prominently in Kierkegaard's books.

The central issue, as we might have suspected, was a fear that the dialectic of inwardness would be either toned down or eliminated altogether, thus making it easy for one to be an individual and a Christian.

> Since we are accustomed to be Christians as a matter of course and to be called Christians, the incongruity emerges that views of life which are much lower than Christianity are propagated within Christianity and have proved more pleasing to men (i.e. to Christians), as naturally is the case, because Christianity is the more difficult, and these views have been acclaimed as higher discoveries which surpass Christianity pure and simple.[1]

[1] Kierkegaard, *Concluding Unscientific Postscript*, p. 521.

The three outcasts, of course, can be reduced to one common denominator, namely, spiritual complacency.

> The speculative philosopher . . . proposes to contemplate Christianity from the philosophical standpoint. It is a matter of indifference to him whether anyone accepts it or not; such anxieties are left to the theologues and laymen. . . . The philosopher contemplates Christianity for the sake of interpenetrating it with his speculative thought; aye, with his genuinely speculative thought.[2]

All of this seems to follow with considerable force. By this we mean that it is impossible to relate subjectivity and truth without at the same time rejecting those positions which develop a view of truth which has no relation to subjectivity.

Even though spiritual complacency is the one common element which runs through speculation, Hegelianism, and objectivity, and even though a discussion of these three positions will necessarily involve a certain amount of repetition, we would do Kierkegaard an injustice, were we to gloss over the types of spiritual complacency which he himself dreaded.

A. *Speculation*

Since Kierkegaard was an expert in the use of pseudonyms, certainly he would be among the first to step forward and defend the *expediency* of speculation. He was concerned because he felt that speculation had drifted away from its true purpose. It was like the money-changer in the New Testament. As long as the speculator kept his trade away from the steps of the temple, he had every right to defend his methodology. "All honor to philosophy, all praise to everyone who brings a genuine devotion to its service."[3] The difficulty, however, was that the money-changer returned to the temple steps as soon as the followers of inwardness left. He had to be driven away; otherwise the temple would no longer be a fit place for the assembly of existentially committed lives.

This helps explain the ambivalence in Kierkegaard's writings.

[2] *Ibid.*, p. 51.
[3] *Ibid.*, p. 54.

On the one hand, he was highly skilled in the use of reason (or understanding), while, on the other hand, he was passionately dedicated to the conviction that human reason, whenever it exceeds its rightful limits, is as devastating a foe of faith as Christian commitment can encounter. When Kierkegaard clashed with rational speculation, therefore, he was merely trying to do his best to show that the rightful limits of human reason had been exceeded. In other words a speculator conveniently avoids the dialectic of inwardness by resorting to "if . . . then" hypotheses. Kierkegaard had no patience with such a strategy.[4]

Let us illustrate what we mean by the use of hypothesis as a substitute for being. Suppose a conversation happened to turn to what it would be like, were a person to disrobe and dive into a cold pool of water. Speculation would rest satisfied by an appeal to a rationally guided exercise of imagination. It would ask what would happen *if* there were a cold pool of water, and *if* there were a person who was willing to dive into the water, and *if* this person finally did what he said he was willing to do. After imagination had rendered its verdict, the speculator could return home without as much as dipping his foot into the cold water.

Therefore, if an existentially committed life will not rest until possibility converts to actuality, a speculator is content with possibility. This is a very important distinction; for whereas the existentialist passionately struggles to make good his responsibilities as an individual and a Christian, a speculator is content to hypothesize.

> With what one might call the inward work philosophy has nothing whatever to do, but the inward work is the genuine life of freedom. Philosophy regards the outward work, and this it does not see in isolation but as it is absorbed into and transformed by the world-historical process.[5]

[4] This viewpoint will seem rash unless it is deliberately interpreted within the context of Kierkegaard's vocation — that of making it difficult to become an individual and a Christian. Legitimate spheres of speculation (such as mathematics) are *not* being challenged.

[5] Kierkegaard, *Either/Or*, II, 147.

It now is clear that Kierkegaard interpreted speculation as a rational expedient by which a person supposed he could pass from thought to factual reality without meeting any spiritual or ethical conditions. Consequently, when speculation declared rather poetically that the order and nature of mind is the same as the order and nature of things, Kierkegaard thundered back that this kind of philosophy could never have been conceived unless a serious rational error had first been made. A speculator may be a person with a richly endowed mind, but this does not justify his tendency to ignore the critical difference between *factual* and *ideal* being. To begin with, the difference does *not* turn on the presence or absence of being. Kierkegaard is very emphatic at this point.

> What is lacking here is a distinction between factual being and ideal being. . . . A fly, when it exists, has as much being as God. . . . Factual existence is wholly indifferent to any and all variations in essence, and everything that exists participates without petty jealousy in being, and participates in the same degree. Ideally to be sure, the case is quite different. *But the moment I speak of being in the ideal sense I no longer speak of being, but of essence.* Highest ideality has this necessity and therefore it is. But this its being is identical with its essence; such being does not involve it dialectically in the determinations of factual existence, since it is; nor can it be said to have more or less of being in relation to other things.[6]

The distinction between factual and ideal being is this: factual being is linked with contingency and becoming, while ideal being is linked with necessity. Hence, it is impossible for a speculator to anticipate the character of factual being by philosophic strategies. The syllogism aptly illustrates the point. It is perfectly logical to say that if all men are mortals, and if Socrates is a man, then Socrates is a mortal. But the difficulty is that this syllogism fails to give the slightest proof that there ever was a man called Socrates.

As we might have expected, Kierkegaard did not miss an

---

[6] Kierkegaard, *Philosophical Fragments*, pp. 32-33n. This is really a tacit version of the ontological argument. How such a concession to rationalism fits in with Kierkegaard's passion for the absurd, is not easy to discover.

opportunity to pour salt into the wound. If it is true that the order and nature of mind is the same as the order and nature of things, then a person need only *think,* not *act.* If he wants to become wealthy, let him merely conceive a room filled with gold. And so it goes: let him think of anything — anything at all — and thinking will make it so.

At this point, however, the speculator intrudes with a word of rebuttal. Although the real is the rational, it is necessary to point out that "this identity must not be understood as applying to [the] existence of an imperfect order, as if, for example, I could produce a rose by thinking it."⁷

But this rejoinder accomplishes nothing; for whenever the speculator succeeds in identifying thought with being, he does so only "because being means in this case the same thing as thought."⁸ This means that rational validity cannot be used as an index to factual being. Therefore, if a speculator continues to speak of the ontological identity of thought and being, he is actually doing no more than repeating the tautology that being is being, or that thought is thought.

> But if being is understood in this manner, the formula becomes a tautology. Thought and being mean one and the same thing, and the correspondence spoken of is merely an abstract self-identity. Neither formula says anything more than that the truth is, so understood as to accentuate the copula: the truth *is,* i.e. the truth is a reduplication. Truth is the subject of the assertion; but the assertion that it is, is the same as the subject; for this being that the truth is said to have is never its own abstract form. . . . Abstract thought may continue as long as it likes to rewrite this thought in varying phraseology, it will never get any farther. As soon as the being which corresponds to the truth comes to be empirically concrete, the truth is put in process of becoming, and is again by way of anticipation the conformity of thought with being. This conformity is actually realized for God, but it is not realized for any existing spirit, who is himself existentially in process of becoming.⁹

By a touch of real genius Kierkegaard insisted that the specu-

---

⁷ Kierkegaard, *Concluding Unscientific Postscript,* p. 293.
⁸ *Idem.*
⁹ *Ibid.,* p. 170.

lator remember that he is a human being, and as a human being he must be true to the realities to which he is already committed by the fact of existence itself. Speculation about ideal being does not cancel out the limitations of factual being. Every human being pays his debt to existence (despite the profundity with which he defines abstraction) by the empirical fact that he exists. After a professor finishes a profound lecture on the universality of the necessary, he then stands in line to buy his lunch or receive his pay check; and thus by his action he refutes the very speculation which forms the heart of his lecture. "It is therefore an existing spirit who is now conceived as raising the question of truth, presumably in order that he may exist in it; but in any case the question is raised by someone who is conscious of being a particular existing human being."[10]

Johannes Climacus, one of Kierkegaard's favorite pseudonyms, was a living person who belonged to the realm of factual being; he was not formed of rational ideals, held together by the laws of logic. As we have previously observed, a living person cannot pass from potentiality to actuality until the specific conditions of selfhood — love's attributes — are mediated in the instant by passionate decision. "Since man is a synthesis of the temporal and the eternal, the happiness that the speculative philosopher may enjoy will be an illusion, in that he desires in time to be merely eternal. . . . Higher than this speculative happiness, therefore, is the infinite passionate interest in a personal eternal happiness. It is higher because it is truer, because it definitely expresses the synthesis."[11]

Hence, in a very able manner, yet in a manner which is neither uniquely new nor uniquely creative, Kierkegaard contends that a *toto caelo* difference exists between the rational necessity of speculation and the contingency of the living person. While necessity *must* be, contingency *may* be. The Christian should not be ashamed that his essence is federated with becoming, for a rejection of becoming is equal to a rejection of factual being.

[10] *Idem.*
[11] *Ibid.*, p. 54.

> Can the necessary come into existence? Becoming is a change; but the necessary cannot undergo any change, since it is always related to itself, and related to itself in the same manner. All coming into being is a kind of *suffering,* and the necessary cannot suffer; it cannot suffer the suffering of the actual, which is that the possible (not only the excluded possibility, but also the accepted possibility) reveals itself as nothing the moment it becomes actual; for the possible is annihilated in the actual. Everything that comes into being proves precisely by coming into being that it is not necessary; for the necessary is the only thing that cannot come into being, because the necessary is.[12]

By way of summary, that which *must* be can have neither a first beginning, a present becoming, nor a future *telos*. But that which *may* be forms an entirely different order, and Kierkegaard is primarily concerned with the elements which make up this second order; for it would be pointless to speak of existential responsibility when things are necessary.

> Necessity stands entirely by itself. Nothing ever comes into being with necessity; what is necessary never comes into being; nothing becomes necessary by coming into being. Nothing whatever exists because it is necessary; but the necessary is because it is necessary, or because the necessary is. The actual is no more necessary than the possible, for the necessary is absolutely different from both.[13]

Right at this point it may seem that Kierkegaard is trying to have his cake and his penny, too. We are told that the necessary never comes into being, and yet we are told that God came into being when Jesus was born of a virgin. Which is it? *Both* replies Kierkegaard. In fact, that which outrages speculation because of its paradoxical nature is the glory of Christianity. "The characteristic mark of Christianity is the paradox, the absolute paradox. As soon as a so-called Christian speculation annuls the paradox and reduces this characterization to a transient factor, all the spheres are confused."[14]

Behind this defense of paradox is the conviction that the ethical self, the only self capable of *becoming* in a true and

---

[12] Kierkegaard, *Philosophical Fragments,* pp. 60-61.
[13] *Ibid.,* p. 61.
[14] Kierkegaard, *Concluding Unscientific Postscript,* p. 480.

praiseworthy sense, must be shocked out of its native tendency to think more highly of itself than it ought. As long as the self succeeds in perpetuating the illusion that its position in time is nothing but an occasion for speculation, so long will the self remain ignorant of its sin. And this ignorance, in turn, will encourage the self to conceive of God as little more than a cosmic counterpart to human reason. Consistent speculation may not spell the end of *religion,* but it spells the end of the *Christian* religion. "Speculative philosophy (in so far as it does not desire to do away with all religiousness in order to introduce us *en masse* into the promised land of pure being) must consistently hold the opinion that religiousness A is higher than B, since it is the religiousness of immanence."[15]

Kierkegaard was not possessed by a demonic zeal to see how many people he could fill with guilt, and it would be demonic to imply that he was. He stressed the importance of ethical decision because he was convinced that the ethical makes up the very substance of freely motivated being. An individual must *mediate* truth by the manner of his conduct, for it is insufficient to speculate about truth while sitting in a soft chair, puffing a pipe. "For a subjective reflection the truth becomes a matter of appropriation, of inwardness, of subjectivity, and thought must probe more and more deeply into the subject and his subjectivity."[16] Again, "It is a misunderstanding to be concerned about reality from the aesthetic or intellectual point of view. And to be concerned ethically about another's reality is also a misunderstanding, since the only question of reality that is ethically pertinent, is the question of one's own reality."[17] If existentialism has any glory, it certainly is here.

Kierkegaard was wholeheartedly dedicated to the conviction that true ethical (or religious) being has no reality unless the self consciously accepts the kind of risk which speculative reason would spew out as unworthy. Risk is an inseparable part of faith. Speculation remains attractive because of the subtle way that it relieves the self of any element of personal involve-

---

[15] *Ibid.,* p. 496.
[16] *Ibid.,* p. 171.
[17] *Ibid.,* p. 287.

ment. It does this by turning from the ethical to the rational. The dialectic of inwardness is dissolved by the simple expedient of defining man as a rational creature. Kierkegaard realized that he was dealing with high stakes: the gaining or losing of the Christian faith.

> In this transition Christianity makes its start; by proceeding along this path it proves that sin lies in the will, thus attaining the concept of defiance; and then, in order to make the end thoroughly fast, it adjoins to this the dogma of original sin — for, alas, the secret of Speculation's success in comprehending is just this, of sewing without making the end fast and without knotting the thread, and therefore it can marvellously keep on sewing, i.e. keep on pulling the end through. Christianity, on the contrary, fastens the end by means of the paradox.[18]

Behind much of this is the theological assumption that God remains unknown to human reason, both in his eternal essence and in his temporal incarnation. Therefore, when speculation tries to do away with faith, it is actually trying to do away with God, whether it realizes it or not. Kierkegaard was confident that a right use of reason implies an acknowledgement of reason's limitations, thus opening the way for faith.

> What then is the Unknown? It is the limit to which the Reason repeatedly comes, and in so far, substituting a static form of conception for the dynamic, it is the different, the absolutely different. But because it is absolutely different, there is no mark by which it could be distinguished. When qualified as absolutely different it seems on the verge of disclosure, but this is not the case; for the Reason cannot even conceive an absolute unlikeness. The Reason cannot negate itself absolutely, but uses itself for the purpose, and thus conceives only such an unlikeness within itself as it can conceive by means of itself; it cannot absolutely transcend itself, and hence conceives only such a superiority over itself as it can conceive by means of itself. Unless the Unknown (God) remains a mere limiting conception, the single idea of difference will be thrown into a state of confusion, and become many ideas of many differences.[19]

Much of this is admittedly difficult. But Kierkegaard seems to be saying (1) that man exists, and (2) that only Christianity

---

[18] Kierkegaard, *The Sickness Unto Death*, pp. 150-151.
[19] Kierkegaard, *Philosophical Fragments*, p. 35.

can meaningfully account for this existence. Unlike speculation, for which ". . . thought must be pointed away from the subject. . ."[20] Christianity is ". . . precisely an explanation of how the eternal truth is to be understood in determinations of time by one who as existing is himself in time."[21]

As a final rejoinder the speculator may assert that only by defending the primacy of reason can the "madness" of subjectivity be avoided. Madness implies the want of any sure criteria by which to test the claims of inwardness, and so establish the presence of truth.

In a rather dramatic gesture Kierkegaard refers to the insane man who, on escaping from an asylum, contrives a scheme by which he can prove to others that he is not mad. His wonderful scheme is to repeat a certain objective truth that he has memorized. But to his disappointment, the more he repeats the truth, the more others suspect that he is mad.

Kierkegaard's point is that we must not be hasty in limiting the charge of madness. A philosophy professor is really not much different from the insane man referred to above, for he stands before his class and repeats and repeats objective truths. Ironically, however, he is paid for his much speaking, while the insane man is confined to an institution.

As far as Kierkegaard is concerned, therefore, the real issue is not, who is *mad,* but, who is *madder.* In short, there are types of madness: subjective zeal and objective zeal.

> In the type of madness which manifests itself as an aberrant inwardness, the tragic and the comic is that the something which is of such infinite concern to the unfortunate individual is a particular fixation which does not really concern anybody. In the type of madness which consists in the absence of inwardness, the comic is that though the something which the happy individual knows really is the truth, the truth which concerns all men, it does not in the slightest degree concern the much respected prater. This type of madness is more inhuman than the other. One shrinks from looking into the eyes of a madman of the former type lest one be compelled to plumb there the depths of his delirium; but one dares not look at a madman

[20] Kierkegaard, *Concluding Unscientific Postscript*, p. 171.
[21] *Ibid.*, p. 172.

of the latter type at all, from fear of discovering that he has eyes of glass and hair made from carpet-rags; that he is, in short, an artificial product.[22]

The speculator is a sophisticated madman. He goes about repeating and repeating that the real is the rational, while all the while he is a human being who is motivated more strongly by personal interest than by rational necessity. He is quick to charge followers of subjective truth with madness, but he seems to have no feeling for the degree to which he himself is mad.

B. *Hegelianism*

Kierkegaard is very outspoken in his denunciation of Hegel, and the reason for this is simply the fact that Hegel failed to relate his rational system to the living responsibility of a finite individual.

> The confusion which Hegelian philosophy has brought into personal life is altogether incredible — it is the sad consequence of a philosopher being a hero and yet, from a purely personal point of view, a philistine and a pedant. One thing always escaped Hegel — what it was to live. He could only give a representation of life, and though a master in that art he is quite certainly the most striking contrast to a maieutic thinker.[23]

Since Hegel rose to such philosophic heights, it is only natural that the shadow of Socrates fell across Kierkegaard once again. Even though Socrates was a philosopher, he was not far from the kingdom. "The infinite merit of the Socratic position was precisely to accentuate the fact that the knower is an existing individual, and that the task of existing is his essential task. Making an advance upon Socrates by failing to understand this, is quite a mediocre achievement."[24] Kierkegaard blames Plato for pinning the recollection-principle on Socrates. "By holding Socrates down to the proposition that all knowledge is recollection, he becomes a speculative philosopher instead of an existential thinker, for whom existence is the essential thing. . . . To accentuate existence, which also involves the qualification

---

[22] *Ibid.,* p. 175.
[23] Kierkgaard, *Journals,* 610.
[24] Kierkegaard, *Concluding Unscientific Postscript,* p. 185.

of inwardness, is the Socratic position; the Platonic tendency, on the other hand, is to pursue the lure of recollection and immanence."[25] Kierkegaard assigns Hegel a position next to Plato, for both philosophers disparage the relationship between personal existence and eternal truth. Even though Hegel by chance knew *everything*, while Socrates knew *nothing*, it nonetheless follows that the ignorance of Socrates "if it is to be thoroughly grasped and retained, is more strenuous to carry out than all Hegel's philosophy put together."[26]

With this introductory reference before us, let us proceed by recalling the distinction which Kierkegaard introduced when the question of constructing a "system" was raised. On the one hand, a *logical* system is possible; while, on the other, an *existential* system is impossible. Unless this distinction is borne in mind, Kierkegaard's impatience with Hegel will not be appreciated.

Kierkegaard posited the possibility of a logical system in order that the prerogative of a person to fabricate a hypothetical world view might be guaranteed. When dealing with the Christian position as a problem of thought, therefore, Kierkegaard deliberately set up a logical system. He felt that he had to speak the language of fools as part of the price which had to be paid whenever a serious attempt was made to arouse fools out of their folly. Hence, in the *Philosophical Fragments* he exhibited true genius when he reduced Christianity to a problem of thought. Even though this method was so unworthy of existentialism that it had to be penned under a pseudonym, both the characteristics and purpose of a logical system were convincingly set forth.

Kierkegaard resisted the possibility of an existential system — except for God, who includes all existence within himself — because the living individual, whose task it is to mediate the eternal in time through passionate, ethical decision, is always in the process of becoming, or at least he *should* be. A logical system cannot deal with the state of becoming, since its essence

---

[25] *Ibid.*, pp. 184-185n.
[26] Kierkegaard, *Journals*, 511.

is composed of the necessary and unchanging. The only way to introduce harmony into this conflict is ". . . to relegate thought to the sphere of the possible, the disinterested, the objective, and to assign action to the sphere of the subjective."[27]

But this is precisely what Hegel failed to do — or at least this is the charge leveled by Kierkegaard. Hegel formulated a rationally fixed system which was designed to take in the whole of reality. But the system could *not* take in the existing individual, for such an individual is characterized by moment-by-moment becoming, rather than by logical necessity. Kierkegaard felt that Hegel's failure was as much a joke as it was tragedy. Whoever is not able to see humor in the following passage ought to consult a doctor, for it is genuinely funny to have an absolute, rational system drawn up by a finite human being.

> One must therefore be very careful in dealing with a philosopher of the Hegelian school, and, above all, to make certain of the identity of the being with whom one has the honor to discourse. Is he a human being, an existing human being? Is he himself *sub specie aeterni*, even when he sleeps, eats, blows his nose, or whatever else a human being does? Is he himself the pure "I am I"? This is an idea that has surely never occurred to any philosopher; but if not, how does he stand existentially related to this entity, and through what intermediate determinations is the ethical responsibility resting upon him as an existing individual suitably respected? Does he in fact exist? And if he does, is he then not in process of becoming? . . . Was he born *sub specie aeterni*, and has he lived *sub specie aeterni* ever since, so that he cannot even understand what I am asking about, never having had anything to do with the future, and never having experienced any decision? In that case I readily understand that it is not a human being I have the honor to address. But this does not quite end the matter; for it seems to me a very strange circumstance that such mysterious beings begin to make their appearance. An epidemic of cholera is usually signalized by the appearance of a certain kind of fly not otherwise observable; may it not be the case that the appearance of these fabulous pure thinkers is a sign that some misfortune threatens humanity, as for instance the loss of the ethical and the religious?[28]

[27] Kierkegaard, *Concluding Unscientific Postscript*, p. 302.
[28] *Ibid.*, pp. 271-272.

Once it is clearly understood that only the divine being can actuate an existential system, it necessarily follows that any philosopher who composes a system is a living individual like Kierkegaard himself. Depending upon how much profit this insight has brought, therefore, the dealer in systems can either formulate an ideal world view which takes in the individual just as it takes in everything else, or he can acknowledge that the contingency of the individual invalidates the possibility of an ideal world view. These are harsh alternatives, but there is no *tertium quid*.

> *Either* he can do his utmost to forget that he is an existing individual, by which he becomes a comic figure, since existence has the remarkable trait of compelling an existing individual to exist whether he wills it or not. . . . *Or* he can concentrate his entire energy upon the fact that he is an existing individual. It is from this side, in the first instance, that objection must be made to modern philosophy; not that it has a mistaken presupposition, but that it has a comical presupposition, occasioned by its having forgotten, in a sort of world-historical absent-mindedness, what it means to be a human being. Not indeed, what it means to be a human being in general; for this is the sort of thing that one might even induce a speculative philosopher to agree to; but what it means that you and I and he are human beings, each one for himself.[29]

Since Hegel dedicated himself to the formulation of a logical world view, Kierkegaard was convinced that this dedication was representative of philosophy's repeated effort to pass from the category of rational necessity to the category of contingency and movement in history. Illusion sat on the throne because the individual was dethroned.

> In the construction of a logical system, it is necessary first and foremost to take care not to include in it anything which is subject to an existential dialectic, anything which is, only because it exists or has existed, and not simply because it is. From this it follows quite simply that Hegel's unparalleled discovery, the subject of so unparalleled an admiration, namely, the introduction of movement into logic, is a sheer confusion of logical science; to say nothing of the absence, on every other

[29] *Ibid.*, p. 109.

page, of even so much an effort on Hegel's part to persuade the reader that it is there.[30]

Whenever the claim to an absolute logical system is made, nothing crucial is left for the existing individual. Why, then, bother to go on living? "For suicide is the only tolerable existential consequence of pure thought, when this type of abstraction is not conceived as something merely partial in relation to being human, willing to strike an agreement with an ethical and religious form of personal existence, but assumes to be all and highest."[31] Kierkegaard was by no means justifying suicide as a moral expedient; rather, he was contending that once an absolute system takes over, the kind of passionate decision which the existing individual is left with, is little less than suicide itself. In sum, if we can't *live* with passionate commitment, the least we can do is to *die* with passionate commitment.

Inasmuch as the absolute system is impotent to interpret the most critical phase of factual being, namely, the existing individual, it should be forthrightly resisted as a cheat and a fraud. "The most dangerous form of scepticism is always that which least looks like it. The notion that pure thought is the positive truth for an existing individual, is sheer scepticism, for this positiveness is chimerical."[32] Again, ". . . a philosophy of pure thought is for an existing individual a chimera, if the truth that is sought is something to exist in."[33] It may be quite an accomplishment to summarize a detailed history of China or England; but whenever the nature of the existing individual is either neglected or denied, let the flag of shame be raised high for all to see.

Once again Kierkegaard pressed the terms of his existential methodology into very fruitful service. Beginning with the presupposition that it is impossible to go on living meaningfully

---

[30] *Ibid.*, p. 99. "Let admirers of Hegel keep to themselves the privilege of making him out to be a bungler; an opponent will always know how to hold him in honor, as one who has willed something great, though without having achieved it." *Ibid.*, p. 100n.
[31] *Ibid.*, p. 273.
[32] *Ibid.*, p. 275.
[33] *Idem.*

without passion, he passed swiftly to the conclusion that pure thought, such as Hegel contrived it, is illusory. A living individual has only one consuming interest, and that is himself as a living individual. This consuming interest is *not* that of a system of pure thought, one which is based on little less than abstractions.

> Existence constitutes the highest interest of the existing individual, and his interest in his existence constitutes his reality. What reality is, cannot be expressed in the language of abstraction. . . . Abstract thought considers both possibility and reality, but its concept of reality is a false reflection, since the medium within which the concept is thought is not reality, but possibility.[34]

Behind Kierkegaard's impatience with the Hegelian system lay the relevant but somewhat repetitious fear that the substance of the ethical life would be destroyed. Hegel, as Kierkegaard interpreted him, perceived everything *sub specie aeternitatis*. The eternal, however, is comprised of changeless necessity. But meaningful ethical decisions are linked with the contingency of change; therefore, Hegel did not embrace a workable ethical theory.

Indeed, Kierkegaard conceded that Hegel loosely and generously spoke of history, becoming, and change, conditions which seem ideal for the fulfilment of ethical choices. But he was able to do this (so Kierkegaard was convinced) by paying insufficient attention to the essence of a logically necessary system. If the real is the rational, then the condition of becoming — a condition which is other than rational and which is *sine qua non* for ethical decision — is not possible.

Hegel made no small use of the dialectic, to be sure; in fact, the thesis of the dialectic, which eventually leads to the antithesis and the synthesis, seems to involve a moving relationship; but it only happens to take place in the mind. *Being* empties into *nothing* or converts to *becoming*, only within the neat but unempirical conditions of rational thought. Hence the root

---

[34] *Ibid.*, p. 279. This rare grasp of human self-love is one of the reasons why Kierkegaard towered so high in his defense of the biblical ethic that we should love our neighbors as we love ourselves. Here the eternal invades time with tremendous ethical force.

objection to Hegel's system is that everything from the analysis of basic being on up to the Absolute, is an achievement of formal logic. The overcoming quality of the synthesis is that higher rational unity in which the contradictions which relate the thesis to the antithesis are mediated. In sum, the paradoxes resolved in the Absolute are finally dissolved, and the true is the whole. No task of mediation is left for the existing individual.

It seems, then, that the dialectic of Hegel was carried too far to suit Kierkegaard; for the dialectic not only set up the problem of living, but it also mediated the contradictions.

> Verily, we do not need Hegel to tell us that relative contradictions can be mediated, since the fact that they can be separated is found in the ancients; and personality will protest in all eternity against the proposition that absolute contradictions can be mediated (and this protest is incommensurable with the mediation's assertion) it will repeat its *immortal* dilemma through all eternity: to be or not to be, that is the question (Hamlet).[35]

Whereas Hegel strove to mediate everything in the category of both/and, Kierkegaard, defending both the primacy and the responsibility of the ethical individual, turned to the price-exacting category of either/or. This is why Kierkegaard saw no possibility of harmonizing the ethos of Christianity with that of Hegelianism. In religiousness B (Christianity or paradoxical religiousness) the existing individual performs the act of mediation through ethical, existential decision, whereas in Hegelianism the Absolute harmonizes everything. "If Christianity is the opposite of speculation it is also the opposite of mediation, the latter being a category of speculative thought; what then can it mean to mediate them? But what is the opposite of mediation? It is the absolute paradox."[36]

A final way to express the destruction of ethics in a *sub specie aeternitatis* system is by exposing Hegel's futile effort to include the *future*. Existential choice is so intimately involved in ethical choice that a passionate regard for decision makes the whole

---

[35] Kierkegaard, *Journals*, 286.
[36] Kierkegaard, *Concluding Unscientific Postscript*, p. 338.

future dimension of possibilities turn on the decisions of the present moment. Kierkegaard was convinced that this element of personal creativity made Christianity unique.

> Philosophy . . . . it seems to me to give no answer at all to the question I put to it, for I ask about the future. You, after all, do in a way give an answer, even though it is nonsense. Now I assume that philosophy is in the right, that the principle of contradiction really is annulled, or that the philosophers transcend it every instant in the higher unity which exists for thought. This, however, surely cannot hold with respect to the future, for the oppositions must first be in existence before I can mediate them. But if the oppositions are there, then there must be an either/or.[37]

As we might have expected, Kierkegaard's critique of Hegel is generously sprinkled with elements of satire. *"How does the System begin with the immediate? That is to say, does it begin with it immediately?"*[38] Since a philosopher faces infinite possibilities right from the start, he either settles for a starting point which happens to attract him, or he must face the prospect of dying before he even begins. The same is true with ending a system: either an arbitrary end is chosen or the system continues enlarging forever. Kierkegaard is worthy of being quoted extensively here.

> What is the implication involved in speaking of a bad infinite? The implication is, that I hold some person responsible for refusing to end the reflective process. And this means, does it not, that I require him to do something? But as a genuinely speculative philosopher I assume, on the contrary, that reflecttion ends itself. If that is the case, why do I make any demand upon the thinker? And what is it that I require of him? I ask him for a resolve. And in so doing, I do well, for in no other way can the process of reflection be halted. But a philosopher is never justified, on the other hand, in playing tricks on people, asserting one moment that the reflective process halts itself and comes to an end in an absolute beginning; and the next moment proceeding to mock a man whose only fault is that

---

[37] Kierkegaard, *Either/Or*, II, 144. This assertion, that the principle of contradiction is annulled, is wide of the mark; for apart from the validity of this principle, Kierkegaard himself could not meaningfully assert that the principle is annulled.
[38] Kierkegaard, *Concluding Unscientific Postscript*, p. 101.

he is stupid enough to believe the first assertion, mocking him, so as to help him to arrive in this manner at an absolute beginning, which hence seems to be achieved in two different ways. But if a resolution of the will is required to end the preliminary process of reflection, the presuppositionless character of the System is renounced. Only when reflection comes to a halt can a beginning be made, and reflection can be halted only by something else, and this something else is something quite different from the logical, being a resolution of the will. Only when the beginning, which puts an end to the process of reflection, is a radical breach of such a nature that the absolute beginning breaks through the continued infinite reflection, then only is the beginning without presuppositions.[39]

Kierkegaard placed Hegel in a company of philosophers who are frantically struggling to complete their systems, but who sadly forget what it means to be part of the human race. They imagine that they are more competent than they really are, for "When they publish their epitomes they say nothing about anything being lacking. Thus they lead their readers to suppose that everything is complete, unless they write for those better informed than they are themselves, which would doubtless seem unthinkable to sytematists."[40]

In sum, the one who composes the system is not part of the system. Nothing can dethrone the primacy of the ethical life, no matter how rationally tight the system may be. Existentialism towers over pure thought. "A persistent striving to realize a system is . . . still a striving. . . ."[41]

But before we leave this topic, we must, in fairness, point out that Kierkegaard learned a good deal from the dialectic by Hegel. "He translated the hardest passages into Danish, in order to make them clearer to himself, and he read and re-read the *Logic* [of Hegel] over and over again. Both his philosophical style and his terminology show the influence of Hegel."[42] Lowrie has actually uncovered a laudatory passage which was originally intended to be inserted as a footnote in the *Concluding Unscientific Postscript*.

[39] *Ibid.*, p. 103.
[40] *Ibid.*, p. 98.
[41] *Idem.*
[42] Swenson, *Something About Kierkegaard*, p. 11.

> I would here beg the reader's attention to a remark I have often desired to make. Let no one misunderstand me, as though I imagined I were the devil of a thinker who might transform everything. Such thinkers are as remote from me as possible. I cherish a respect for Hegel which is sometimes an enigma to me; I have learnt much from him, and I know that on returning again to him I could still learn much more.[43]

Hegel, we repeat, supplied Kierkegaard with the basic framework of dialectical thinking, namely, the tensional strain of the thesis-antithesis relationship; but Kierkegaard insisted that the tension was mediated by the ethically centered, existing individual, and not by the powers of pure thought.

Kierkegaard broke with Hegel in the conviction that Hegelian logic became quagmired in the slough of *sub specie aeternitatis;* and in this manner the logic found itself on a futile path of trying desperately to handle contingent phenomena. We must not suppose, therefore, that Kierkegaard objected to either the formulation of a logical dialectic or to the claim that such a dialectic must have empirical foundations. His displeasure did not grow out of the feeling that Hegel used logic to set up a problem of thought, but rather that Hegel went on to identify logic with reality itself.

It was only natural that Kierkegaard, in breaking with Hegel, turned for solace to the Socratic emphasis upon the existing individual. Rather than investing pure thought with the authority to mediate the thesis-antithesis principle, the maieutic philosophy taught that the *individual himself* must mediate the synthesis in personal passion. Dialectic is certainly the basis of the ethical life, for without the pointed edges of paradox the existing individual would fail to be suspended in a state of inward, spiritual passion. In an exceedingly relevant passage Kierkegaard makes it clear that existence outside of the dialectic is a soulless way of life.

> What serves to mark the thoroughly cultivated personality is the degree to which the thinking in which he has his daily life has a dialectical character. To have one's daily life in the decisive dialectic of the infinite, and yet continue to live; this

---

[43] Kierkegaard, *Concluding Unscientific Postscript,* p. 558, notes.

is both the art of life and its difficulty. Most men have complacent categories for their daily use, and resort to the categories of the infinite only upon solemn occasions; that is to say, they do not really have them. But to make use of the dialectic of the infinite in one's daily life, and to exist in this dialectic, is naturally the highest degree of strenuousness; and strenuous exertion is again needed to prevent the exercise from deceitfully luring one away from existence, instead of providing a training in existence. It is a well-known fact that a cannonade tends to deafen one to other sounds; but it is also a fact that persistence in enduring it may enable one to hear every word of a conversation as clearly as when all is still. Such is also the experience of one who leads an existence as spirit, intensified by reflection.[44]

The dialectical mediation of eternity in time may be a way of the cross, but it is also a way of virtue. Virtue is formed of acts of self-giving love, and such love is only expressed when the inner man is developed by conscientious choices of what is right. Therefore, when one gives birth to subjective truth, he gives birth to virtue itself. This means that the Kierkegaardian appeal to Socrates was confined to existential insights; he had no sympathy with reminiscence as an expression of mediation. "The individual through strain and suffering becomes what he becomes."[45]

C. *Objectivity*

Since words have a way of deceiving us, it is well that we first try to comprehend the ambiguity in the term, "objectivity." We generally credit something with objective existence if it is "out there," independent of both feeling and opinion. In other words, objectivity in this sense is merely another name for external reality. If this were the way Kierkegaard used the term when he said that Christianity is subjective, the effort of Kierkegaard could be dismissed as mere skepticism.

Therefore, let it be asserted for all to hear that Kierkegaard did *not* separate himself from the traditional orthodox claim that the data of Christianity are objective in the sense of existing

---

[44] *Ibid.,* pp. 79-80n.
[45] Swenson, *op. cit.,* p. 119.

"out there." What disturbed him, rather, was the way professing Christians substituted intellectual assent to these data for the decisive, ethical state of *being* Christians. A datum is objective in the uninteresting sense — on existential criteria, that is — when it can be acknowledged by the existing individual without any accompanying inwardness or spiritual concern. Thus, a pile of rubbish may be considered objective when judged by the standards of common sense. But Kierkegaard would have considered it objective because it is a kind of "out-there-ness" which is impotent to shock the existing individual into a state of responsible inwardness.

In like manner, the absolute paradox (the incarnation, that is) may have existed as an historical fact, and thus be objective according to the common sense norm. But according to the special usage set forth by Kierkegaard, the objective is the converse of the subjective, and the subjective is character change, spiritual development, personal responsibility, and inner concern. "Here we are again reminded of my thesis that subjectivity is truth; for an objective truth is like the eternity of abstract thought, extraneous to the movement of existence."[46]

> But . . . suppose that Christianity is subjectivity, an inner transformation, an actualization of inwardness, and that only two kinds of people can know anything about it: those who with an infinite passionate interest in an eternal happiness base this their happiness upon their believing relationship to Christianity, and those who with an opposite passion, but in passion, reject it — the happy and the unhappy lovers. . . . Now if Christianity is essentially something objective, it is necessary for the observer to be objective. But if Christianity is essentially subjectivity, it is a mistake for the observer to be objective.[47]

It is necessary that we belabor this point, for the dialectic of inwardness is sustained by the fact (objective and historical in the non-Kierkegaardian sense) that the eternal God assumed the form of a finite person, and thus became the God-man at a particular point in time. "The historical assertion is that the Deity, the Eternal, came into being at a definite moment in

---

[46] Kierkegaard, *Concluding Unscientific Postscript*, p. 278.
[47] *Ibid.*, p. 51.

time as an individual man."[48] Spiritual passion and wholesouled ethical decision are experienced when the existing individual, by an act of faith, casts himself upon the contradiction involved in basing ". . . an eternal happiness upon the relation to something historical."[49] In other words, "Christianity is an existence-communication which makes the thing of existing paradoxical and difficult to a degree it never was before and never can be outside of Christianity, but it is no short cut to becoming incomparably clever."[50]

Kierkegaard makes his readers work very hard, exactly as he intended; for right after he freely admitted that Christianity is a religion based on historical events, he turned right around and denied that the Christian religion is objective.

> It is subjectivity that Christianity is concerned with, and it is only in subjectivity that its truth exists, if it exists at all; objectively, Christianity has absolutely no existence. If its truth happens to be in only a single subject, it exists in him alone; and there is greater Christian joy in heaven over this one individual than over universal history and the System, which as objective entities are incommensurable for that which is Christian.[51]

Right now we are confronted with a strange paradox; for whereas Kierkegaard was a master in the art of Christian apologetics, he experienced a disappointing bitterness whenever he surveyed the customary goals of apologists. In his estimation there is "only one proof of the truth of Christianity and that, quite rightly, is from the emotions, when the dread of sin and a heavy conscience torture a man into crossing the narrow line between despair bordering upon madness — and Christendom. *There* lies Christianity."[52] It is only natural, therefore, that Kierkegaard resisted the efforts of those who presumed that in establishing the historical data of Christianity (by archaeology, for example), the truth of Christianity was established. Kierkegaard became severe at this point. If a Christian may rest in the

---

[48] *Ibid.*, p. 512.
[49] *Ibid.*, p. 513.
[50] *Ibid.*, p. 501.
[51] *Ibid.*, p. 116.
[52] Kierkegaard, *Journals*, 926.

objectivity of historical facts, rather than undertake the task of mediating Christian truth in his own person, he can eat, drink, and be merry, for the historical data exist "out there" whether he does anything about them or not. The result, according to Kierkegaard, is the annihilation of the existing individual.

In short, the state of subjective truth has no reality until the existing individual perceives a relation between the spiritual happiness of the self and the degree to which the self is passionately committed. For example, if a person knows that he must sit in a particular chair at a particular time, and if he also knows that the chair will either support him or let him fall, depending on how he gives himself to the chair, he will experience more personal passion than he would if he were antecedently assured that the chair will support him no matter how he sits in it. Thus, the more the data "out there" can either make or undo a person, the more one will deem it important that he be correctly related to such data. Mere objective questions, such as whether there are nine or ten square feet of grass in a particular area of the park, are irrelevant; while a passionate concern for things which are external, such as a miser anxiously fingering his money, is idolatry. But when the gaining or losing of eternal happiness is at stake — and Kierkegaard felt certain that only Christianity could confront one with such an option — a maximum of inner passion should be expressed.

This means that the God-man doctrine, no matter how objectively and historically it may be viewed, is useless as a part of the Christian religion until it is passionately perceived as the absolute paradox. Combine all the objective and historical evidences you want, and you will not, according to Kierkegaard, have more than probability or an approximation. "If all the angels in heaven were to put their heads together, they could still bring to pass only an approximation, because an approximation is the only certainty attainable for historical knowledge — but also an inadequate basis for an eternal happiness."[53]

[53] Kierkegaard, *Concluding Unscientific Postscript*, p. 31. The point is not that approximation does not embody risk, for it does. The point is that this degree of risk is insufficient to elicit faith. Only the absolute paradox can dissolve this insufficiency.

Faith would starve on such a diet, for faith is a fruit of inner desperation. Either there is a risk and a leap, or nothing is ventured, so Kierkegaard reasoned. This means that the historian must share the speculator's bench: he is free to define Christianity as a problem of thought, but he has no say in matters of existential truth for such truth is subjectivity.

History, like philosophy, can be learned by rote. Let a divinity student enroll in a course dealing with sacred history. Without deep, inner passion the course will be nothing but a series of routine lectures and assignments. The student may jot down notes; he may yawn frequently; and then, subjectively unedified, though filled with pride by supposing that he is a a wiser person as a result of the discipline, he zips up his notebook and goes to the student commons for coffee. He may receive an A for the course, and still not possess a single grain of faith.

Once Kierkegaard aroused the needed momentum, he did not end his disparagement of historical evidences until he outraged common sense. Because such evidences are so external, he concluded that they stand in the way of an individual's coming to himself inwardly. It requires great faith to resist the temptation of objective complacency. Historical evidences may be compared to the possession of riches: it is easier for a camel to pass through the eye of a needle than for the man who reposes in historical evidences to enter into the existential kingdom of heaven. When knowledge is confused with faith, a great personal disaster follows.

> ... in this objectivity one tends to lose that infinite personal interestedness in passion which is the condition of faith, the *ubique et nusquam* [the everywhere and nowhere] in which faith can come into being. Has anyone who previously had faith gained anything with respect to its strength and power? No, not in the least. Rather is it the case that in this voluminous knowledge, this certainty that lurks at the door of faith and threatens to devour it, he is in so dangerous a situation that he will need to put forth much effort in great fear and trembling, lest he fall a victim to the temptation to confuse knowledge with faith. While faith has hitherto had a profitable schoolmaster in the existing uncertainty, it would have in the new certainty its most dangerous enemy. For if passion is eliminated, faith no longer

exists, and certainty and passion do not go together. Whoever believes that there is a God and an over-ruling providence finds it easier to preserve his faith, easier to acquire something that definitely is faith and not an illusion, in an imperfect world where passion is kept alive, than in an absolutely perfect world. In such a world faith is unthinkable.[54]

On first reading it seems that Kierkegaard destroyed Christianity by trying to separate it from historical evidences. If inner passion can do without evidences, can't faith just as easily do without Jesus Christ?

Kierkegaard might reply that historical evidences, though they may not serve as a basis of faith, nevertheless need not be totally rejected; for they, like riches, may be properly used in the existential kingdom. In reacting against dead orthodoxy, there is little doubt that Kierkegaard went too far. But his general goal had many excellent elements in it, even though he did not always reach his goal.

Let us now examine Kierkegaard's attitude toward apologetics a bit more carefully. He felt that concern for proof of Christianity was a clear sign of unbelief. If a Christian believed, he would not need proof; and if he sought proof, he would show that he does not believe. "When faith thus begins to lose its passion, when faith begins to cease to be faith, then a proof becomes necessary so as to command respect from the side of unbelief."[55] Since Kierkegaard was convinced that apologetics is aimed at removing all the risk involved in becoming a Christian, he concluded that there were few more serious hindrances to the development of true, spiritual Christianity than apologetics; when the church began its witness to the world, instead of simply ignoring the accusation of the pagans, the apologists rushed forward to establish the truth of Christianity in an objective manner. Kierkegaard felt that these apologists tried to lower Christianity to standards which would be acceptable to the pagans. Succeeding apologists followed the same procedure down through the ages: whenever doubt arose, they contrived

[54] *Ibid.*, pp. 30-31.
[55] *Ibid.*, p. 31.

new proofs, not realizing the degree to which such proofs were proofs of doubts.

> So some doubted. But then again there were some who sought by reasons to refute doubt. Really, however, the situation is this: the first thing was that they sought by reasons to prove the truth of Christianity, or to adduce reason in support of it. And these reasons — they begat doubt, and doubt became the stronger. For the proof of Christianity really consists in "following". That they did away with. So they felt the need of reasons; but these reasons, or the fact that there are reasons, is already a sort of doubt — and so doubt arose and thrived upon the reasons. They did not observe that the more reasons one adduces, the more one nourished doubt and the stronger it becomes, that to present doubt with reasons with the intent of slaying it is like giving to a hungry monster one wants to be rid of the delicious food it likes best.[56]

Kierkegaard advised Christians to refrain from rationally disputing with pagans, and in place of this the pagans should be told to follow Christ. A Christian may set up Christianity as a problem of thought, but he must not give the impression that one can enter the kingdom apart from a subjective leap of faith. The early believers who followed were not plagued by doubt. "And why not? First of all, because their lives were too full of effort, too much sacrificed in daily suffering, to be able to sit in idleness and deal with reasons and doubts, odds or evens."[57] The task of seeing subjective truth is so demanding that any Christian who takes it seriously will have little or no time for anything else.

The apologists failed to do justice to paradox. On the one hand, faith confronts paradox because a Christian must base his eternal happiness upon historical probability; while on the other, the very fact of the incarnation is an absolute paradox, quite offensive to the canons of reason, for the whole God became a whole human being in a given moment of time. It is strange, therefore, that the apologists marched boldly forward to defend the rationality, and thus the general acceptability, of the Christian faith. "For the defense wishes out of the goodness of

---

[56] Kierkegaard, *For Self-Examination and Judge for Yourselves!*, p. 88.
[57] *Idem*.

its heart, to take the possibility of offense away."[58] As far as Kierkegaard was concerned, this did it; for Christianity without rational offense is no longer Christianity. "Take away from Christianity the possibility of offense . . . and then lock the churches, the sooner the better, or make them into recreation centers which stand open all day."[59]

The apologist firmly believes that it is easier to become a Christian when the weight of probable evidence is more in his favor than against him, while Kierkegaard vehemently disagreed. In the *Philosophical Fragments* Kierkegaard contended that the first generation of Christians had no advantage over the last. If there were an advantage to living at *one* time in history rather than another, then the accident which forms the advantage would displace the office of faith, and Christianity as inwardness would fall by the wayside. True faith, as has been stressed, does not rest on rationally probable evidences. ". . . to make such an assertion about faith is to slander it."[60]

In attacking the apologetic proofs for God, Kierkegaard rises to unusual heights. He summarizes his objections in a manner not unlike that of David Hume. Since the world is finite, therefore God, who is infinite, cannot be deduced from the world. Moreover, there is no evidence that the possibility of a finite God ever attracted Kierkegaard. Again, "objective dread," Kierkegaard's description of the problem of evil, receives very little treatment in the total literature. Not only is Kierkegaard concerned with spiritual inwardness, rather than objective nature, but he presupposes that God is wholly other than the world. Such divine transcendence and sovereignty must be preserved in order that the incarnation might be nothing less than the *absolute paradox*. To guarantee that the absolute paradox will serve as a perpetual basis for subjective truth, therefore, all apologetic zeal to prove God's existence must be terminated. A human being must live either for or against God, giving up the various attempts to settle the question of God's existence by rational disputation. "If God does not exist it would of course

---

[58] Kierkegaard, *Works of Love*, p. 162.
[59] *Ibid.*, pp. 162-163.
[60] Kierkegaard, *Philosophical Fragments*, p. 79.

be impossible to prove it; and if he does exist it would be folly to attempt it."[61] There is only one way to advance evidences for the divine existence, and that is by taking God seriously enough to mediate God's love in time. All other proofs are void of the very existential element which makes them valid.

> . . . oh, these proofs which are advanced for the truth of Christianity, these devilish learned and profound and perfectly convincing proofs which have filled folios, upon which "Christendom" plumes itself as the State does the army, what do they all amount to in comparison with . . . a living, and the possibility of a career thrown into the bargain?[62]

If a Christian wishes to clarify the reality of the eternal God in time, let him desist from constructing rational proofs, and let him commence loving his neighbor as himself. ". . . God is love, therefore we can resemble God only in loving . . . when you love your neighbor, then you resemble God."[63]

Kierkegaard *does* deal with proofs for the divine being, but since they are necessarily objective in structure, he looks upon himself as a fool dealing with fools. He attacks the ontological argument, for example, on the charge that it either presupposes the assumption that God already exists, in which case it is not even an argument; or it is agnostic about God's existence, in which case it reduces to plain stupidity. As we have observed in other connections, Kierkegaard will have no part of the effort which tries to pass from rational evidence to objective ("out there") evidence.

> Thus when it is argued that God must possess all perfections, or that the highest being must have all perfections, existence is a perfection; *ergo,* God or the highest being must exist: this entire movement of thought is deceptive. For if God is not really conceived as existing in the first part of the argument, the argument cannot even get started. It would then read about as follows: "A supreme being who does not exist must possess all perfections, including that of existence; *ergo,* a supreme being who does not exist does exist." This would be a strange conclusion. Either the supreme being was non-existent in the

---

[61] *Ibid.,* p. 31.
[62] Kierkegaard, *Attack Upon "Christendom,"* p. 145.
[63] Kierkegaard, *Works of Love,* p. 52.

premises, and came into existence in the conclusion, which is quite impossible; or he was existent in the premises, in which case he cannot come into existence in the conclusion.[64]

If a rational thinker could satisfactorily relate himself to God, both existential suffering and subjective truth would lose their significance, for objectivity would assume the crown.

Kierkegaard is likewise convinced that an appeal to the historical Christ is futile; for Christ, being true man as well as true God, concealed his attributes of deity under the veil of finitude. If his deity had not been veiled, he would not thereby have become an object of personal passion, for God is without parts and passions. "And so unrecognizableness, the absolute unrecognizableness, is this: being God, to be also an individual man."[65] Christ disclosed the essence of God by his consistent love. But this did not satisfy many of those who beheld Christ's works of love, for they wanted to behold God directly. "Direct recognizableness is precisely the characteristic of the pagan god."[66] If Christ had openly unveiled the attributes of deity, the very purpose of the incognito would have been nullified, and the point to the maieutic method would have been terminated.

An element of culpability, according to Kierkegaard, must be shared by both apologists and preachers, for they join in the futile effort of showing that God and man have so much in common that a rational bridge can be built from man to God.[67]

> But take away the possibility of offence, as they have done in Christendom, and the whole of Christianity is direct communication; and then Christianity is done away with, for it has become an easy thing, a superficial something which neither wounds nor heals profoundly enough; it is the false invention of human sympathy which forgets the infinite qualitative difference between God and man.[68]

---

[64] Kierkegaard, *Concluding Unscientific Postscript*, p. 298.
[65] Kierkegaard, *Training in Christianity*, p. 127.
[66] *Ibid.*, p. 135.
[67] It is difficult to see how this charge fits in with the admission that by an existential manifestation of love a Christian temporally discloses the eternal essence of God.
[68] Kierkegaard, *Training in Christianity*, p. 139.

Again,

> And something like this, Christianity has always understood by faith. The God-Man must require faith and must refuse direct communication. In a certain sense He can do no otherwise, and He would do no otherwise. As God-Man He is qualitatively different from every other man and therefore must refuse direct communication, He requires faith, requires that He become the *object of faith*.[69]

When an apologist persists in his conviction that he can begin with a human being and work his way up to God, he only adds new pathos to what is already a pathetic situation. By collecting footprints in the sand an apologist may establish the existence of either a man or an animal; but such a method will fail one in his search for God in Christ. If God is merely a rational extension of man, he is not God at all.

> If God and man resemble one another to that degree, if they have that degree of kinship, and thus essentially are included in the same quality, the conclusion, "*ergo* it was God", is nevertheless humbug; for if God is nothing else but that, then God doesn't exist at all. But if God exists, and consequently is distinguished by an infinite difference of quality from all that it means to be a man, then neither can I nor anybody else, by beginning with the assumption that He [Christ] was a man, arrive in all eternity at the conclusion, "therefore it was God". Everyone who has the least dialectical training can easily perceive that the whole argument about consequences is incommensurable with the decision of the question whether it is God, and that this decisive question is presented to man in an entirely different form: whether he will believe that He is what He said He was; or whether he will not believe.[70]

Despite the difficulties which arise, Kierkegaard has developed a magnificent insight at this point. We are not going too far when we contend that Kierkegaard is the zenith of existentialism. If a tree is worthy of aesthetic admiration, a dog of personal affection, and a person of self-giving love, then the only worthy relation that a human being can have to God is worship. The gap between one man and another may be great, but it can be

[69] *Ibid.*, p. 142.
[70] *Ibid.*, p. 31.

filled by deeds of kindness and charity. But the gap between God and man is infinite; therefore, nothing but worship comprises the correct decorum of man whenever a relationship to God is established. *"Worship* is the maximum expression for the God-relationship of a human being, and hence also for his likeness with God, because the qualities are absolutely different."[71]

The proper Christian order of living is, once again, not unlike that followed by the sage of Athens, Socrates.

> He always presupposes God's existence, and under this presupposition seeks to interpenetrate nature with the idea of purpose. Had he been asked why he pursued this method, he would doubtless have explained that he lacked the courage to venture out upon so perilous a voyage of discovery without having made sure of God's existence behind him.[72]

Objective probing is too non-existential to be of help, for man requires an inner assurance of God's existence before he is able to commit himself to anything which involves the being or non-being of the self.

Spiritual passion displaces objectivity, contends Kierkegaard, only when the self comes to itself and inwardly realizes that its claim to self-sufficiency is false and deceiving at every point. Dependence upon God, therefore, is the only meaningful alternative to despair.

> In this manner God certainly becomes a postulate, but not in the otiose manner in which this word is commonly understood. It becomes clear rather that the only way in which an existing individual comes into relation with God, is when the dialectical contradiction brings his passion to the point of despair, and helps him to embrace God with the "category of despair" (faith). Then the postulate is so far from being arbitrary that it is precisely a life-necessity. It is then not so much that God is a postulate, as that the existing individual's postulation of God is a necessity.[73]

It seems that the need for a daily assurance of God is like the nourishment required by the arteries of the body: unless it is

---

[71] Kierkegaard, *Concluding Unscientific Postscript*, p. 369.
[72] Kierkegaard, *Philosophical Fragments*, pp. 34-35.
[73] Kierkegaard, *Concluding Unscientific Postscript*, p. 179n.

possessed, motivation and power to do anything else worth while are wanting. God is instantly real when a man lets go of his self-sufficiency and learns to depend completely upon the infinite. ". . . freedom is the true wonderful lamp; when a man rubs it with ethical passion, God comes into being for him."[74]

When a philosopher presumes that by an objective refutation of the divine existence, the basis of faith is gone, he has, in Kierkegaard's opinion, sadly missed the point. The *absence* of a theoretical support of faith is no more damaging than the *presence* of a theoretical support. Once again Socratic ignorance is much closer to Christianity than the objective claims of the wisest philosopher.

> . . . Christianity teaches that everything Christian exists only for faith; for this reason precisely it wills to be a Socratic, a God-fearing ignorance, which by ignorance defends faith against speculation, keeping watch to see that the deep gulf of qualitative distinction between God/and man may be firmly fixed, as it is in the paradox and in faith, lest God/and man, still more dreadfully than ever it occurred in paganism, might in a way, *philosophice, poetice,* etc., coalesce into one . . . in the System.[75]

The final attack on objectivity is the established institution, to wit, the church. Kierkegaard was righteously indignant when he contemplated the religious status quo in Copenhagen. The church had become a stumblingblock to subjective passion by making it easy for one to become a Christian. The objective creeds, the ecclesiastical ritual, and the hierarchical orders — all stood in the way of inwardness. "My father has told me so, the church records attest it, I have a certificate, and so forth. Oh, yes, my mind is at rest."[76]

Central to the church is doctrine. But doctrine is a rational summary which can be carried in one's pocket; it can be memorized by rote. "Christianity is therefore not a doctrine, but the fact that God has existed."[77] An objective resting in either the church or in the doctrine is both demonic and trifling. ". . . it is

[74] *Ibid.,* p. 124.
[75] Kierkegaard, *The Sickness Unto Death,* p. 161.
[76] Kierkegaard, *Concluding Unscientific Postscript,* p. 43.
[77] *Ibid.,* p. 291.

just as impossible to be mirrored in an objective doctrine as to be mirrored in a wall."[78]

The doctrine of infant baptism conveniently illustrates Kierkegaard's righteous indignation. Infant baptism, while it is universally practiced, is based on such a mechanical, objective ritual that no spiritual inwardness is aroused. The bitter sarcasm in Kierkegaard's *Attack Upon "Christendom"* can be appreciated and partially forgiven when we realize the degree to which Kierkegaard revolted from what he felt was a polished religious system in Copenhagen. Almost anyone could make a dozen Christians more easily than he could make a pound of butter.

> The interest of Christianity, what it wants, is — true Christians. The egoism of the priesthood, both for pecuniary advantage and for the sake of power, stands in relation to — many Christians. "And that's very easily done, it's nothing at all: let's get hold of the children, then each child is given a drop of water on the head — then he is a Christian. If a portion of them don't even get their drop, it comes to the same thing, if only they imagine they got it, and imagine consequently that they are Christians. So in a very short time we have more Christians than there are herring in the herring season, Christians by the millions, and then, by the power of money as well, we are the greatest power the world has ever seen. That thing about eternity is definitely the cleverest of all inventions, when it gets into the right hands, the hands of practical people; for the Founder [Christ], unpractical as he was, had a wrong notion of what Christianity is."[79]

---

[78] Kierkegaard, *For Self-Examination and Judge for Yourselves!*, p. 68.
[79] Kierkegaard, *Attack Upon "Christendom"*, p. 147.

Chapter Six

SUBJECTIVE TRUTH

IF KIERKEGAARD HAD BEEN PRESSED TO EXPLAIN PRECISELY WHAT *affirmative* elements formed his guiding thesis, "Truth is subjectivity," he would not have been lost for an answer; for chief among the conditions of inwardness (subjective truth) are *faith, suffering, hope, and love.* Whenever a Christian honors these conditions in the course of daily life, he can be sure that he is doing all that is required of him.

A. *Faith*

It was almost as difficult for Kierkegaard to define the essence of faith as it was for Aristotle to define the essence of God. Not only is faith the leading existential determinant, but it occupies such an important position in Kierkegaard's over-all world view that it seems to be the condition of inwardness in relation to which all other conditions are defined, but which eludes definition itself. Lowrie speaks very plainly about this issue:

> Do not tell me that what I have said about S. K.'s notion of faith is inadequate. ·I know that very well. How could it be adequate, seeing that S. K., without essential exaggeration, affirms that the immense literature he produced had only one

theme, namely, faith; and that from beginning to end his whole effort had been to define what faith is?[1]

This certainly does not mean that Kierkegaard fled from the task of defining faith. "Faith is: that the self in being itself and in willing to be itself is grounded transparently in God."[2] Next, faith was related to the question of sin in a remarkable way.

> ... too often it has been overlooked that the opposite of sin is not *virtue*, not by any manner of means. This is in part a pagan view which is content with a merely human measure and properly does not know what *sin* is, that all sin is before God. No, the *opposite of sin is faith,* as is affirmed in Rom. 14:23, "whatsoever is not of faith is sin." And for the whole of Christianity it is one of the most decisive definitions that the opposite of sin is not virtue but faith.[3]

Now that a functional relation between faith and sin has been defended, we can profitably hear what Kierkegaard had to say about sin itself.

> Sin is this: *before God, or with the conception of God, to be in despair at not willing to be oneself, or in despair at willing to be oneself.* Thus sin is potentiated weakness or potentiated defiance: sin is the potentiation of despair. The point upon which the emphasis rests is *before God,* or the fact that the conception of God is involved; the factor which dialectically, ethically, religiously, makes "qualified" despair (to use a juridical term) synonymous with sin is the conception of God.[4]

From this it would seem to follow that if sin is a state of despair before God — despair at *not* willing to be oneself or despair at willing to *be* oneself — then faith, which Kierkegaard spoke of as the opposite of sin, is a condition of the self before God in which the self, free from despair, *is* willing to meet the divinely decreed conditions of selfhood.

Or to put the matter another way, it is only by means of such selfhood that the existing individual succeeds in casting off all speculation and objectivity — succeeds in the sense that the

---

[1] Lowrie, *Kierkegaard*, p. 319.
[2] Kierkegaard, *The Sickness Unto Death*, p. 132.
[3] *Idem.*
[4] *Ibid.*, p. 123.

self is overwhelmed by spirit. Since faith teaches the self how to find its essence in the absoluteness of God, the individual at once becomes higher than the universal — the universal, that is, as it is associated with speculation and objectivity.

Still, we are confronted with a new paradox; for how can the individual be higher than the universal in *any* sense?

> The paradox of faith is this, that the individual is higher than the universal, that the individual (to recall a dogmatic distinction now rather seldom heard) determines his relation to the universal by his relation to the absolute, not his relation to the absolute by his relation to the universal. The paradox can also be expressed by saying that there is an absolute duty toward God; for in this relationship of duty the individual as an individual stands related absolutely to the absolute. So when in this connection it is said that it is a duty to love God . . . for if this duty is absolute, the ethical is reduced to a position of relativity.[5]

But if the universal is higher than the individual (on speculative and objective criteria), then it would seem to follow that the existing individual would enjoy a higher place on the scale of reality than existentialism itself can defend. This might have put Kierkegaard in a difficult position, but it did not. As we have mentioned before, Kierkegaard had no objection to speculation and objectivity, as long as they confined themselves to such non-existential areas as formal logic, mathematics, or semantics. But when speculation and objectivity reached out and took in reality, thus swallowing up the existing individual, Kierkegaard was righteously indignant. The moment a Christian is either absorbed into the universal or may be known through the universal, the validity of the thesis, "Truth is subjectivity," is denied, and we are again back in the environment of personal complacency.

Kierkegaard made no small use of the account of faith in Abraham, for the account combines a rejection of immanence with an absolute determination to live before God. Every indication suggests that the *religious* man supercedes the *ethical* man, although strangely enough Kierkegaard made no con-

---

[5] Kierkegaard, *Fear and Trembling*, p. 105.

vincing apologetic effort to harmonize this with his emphasis elsewhere that the *ethical* man is the *real* man. Kierkegaard does propose, however, that in the exercise of religious faith it may at times become necessary to turn against the ethical. "From this ... it does not follow that the ethical is to be abolished, but it acquires an entirely different expression, the paradoxical expression — that, for example, love to God may cause the knight of faith to give his love to his neighbor the opposite expression to that which, ethically speaking, is required by duty."[6]

In the story of Abraham the ingredients which make up a life of faith are ideally blended. When Abraham learned what it meant to live before God (*coram Deo*), absolute devotion to the details of ethics was replaced by absolute devotion to the will of God. This meant that Abraham discovered what it meant to be an existing individual, that is, to *be* because of his relation to God. He was obedient to the word of God, as God commanded him to leave his kindred and his father's house, even though he was at the great age of seventy-five. Though he was rich in cattle, silver, and gold, God meant all to him. Leaving Haran called for a crucifixion of the understanding; for judged by the wisdom of this world, the journey to the promised land was an act of unadulterated foolishness.

> By faith Abraham went out from the land of his fathers and became a sojourner in the land of promise. He left one thing behind, took one thing with him: he left his earthly understanding behind and took faith with him — otherwise he would not have wandered forth but would have thought this unreasonable. By faith he was a stranger in the land of promise, and there was nothing to recall what was dear to him, but by its novelty everything tempted his soul to melancholy yearning — and yet he was God's elect, in whom the Lord was well pleased![7]

The more completely Abraham surrendered himself to God, the more his passion for following the will of God took on new strength. If we may use a figure of speech, Abraham became an obedient steed leaping to attention at the slightest command from God.

[6] *Idem.*
[7] *Ibid.*, p. 20.

It doesn't take much imagination to see that the most difficult element in Abraham's journey of faith came when God issued a command which was in direct opposition to the ethical criteria which Abraham himself honored, as did others. "After these things God tested Abraham, and said to him, 'Abraham!' And he said, 'Here am I.' He said, 'Take your son, your only son Isaac, whom you love, and go to the land of Moriah, and offer him there as a burnt offering upon one of the mountains of which I shall tell you.' "[8] Abraham might have questioned the right of God to issue such a command, had he concentrated on the duty of fulfilling ethics, rather than on the duty of fulfilling the will of God. This test of faith contains a serious moral and theological problem, to be sure. *Does* a father have a right to kill his son? Abraham was a father, and he knew that the answer was *no*. But Abraham also knew that God, the creator and sustainer of all life, had privileges which could not be transferred to human fathers. Therefore, the will of God must come before the claims of ethics; otherwise faith is dormant just when it should be active.

> . . . Abraham believed and did not doubt, he believed the preposterous. If Abraham had doubted — then he would have done something else, something glorious; for how could Abraham do anything but what is great and glorious! He would have marched up to Mount Moriah, he would have cleft the fire-wood, lit the pyre, drawn the knife — he would have cried out to God, 'Despise not this sacrifice, it is not the best thing I possess, that I know well, for what is an old man in comparison with the child of promise; but it is the best I am able to give Thee. Let Isaac never come to know this, that he may console himself with his youth.' He would have plunged the knife into his own breast. He would have been admired in the world, and his name would not have been forgotten; but it is one thing to be admired, and another to be the guiding star which saves the anguished.[9]

Not *fully* knowing, and not *clearly* seeing, but always drawing on faith, Abraham did not stagger before the divine command. "He knew that it was God the Almighty who was trying him, he knew that it was the hardest sacrifice that could be required

---

[8] Genesis 22:1-2.
[9] Kierkegaard, *Fear and Trembling*, p. 26.

of him; but he knew also that no sacrifice was too hard when God required it — and he drew the knife."[10] Dread, the dizziness of freedom, did not overcome Abraham. The sacrifice of Isaac was a direct offense to ethics; but since *God* commanded the sacrifice, that settled the question. This illustrates the kind of peace which courageous faith brings, but which a want of such faith cannot. Abraham fully realized that nothing worth having would be gained by disputing with God; so, he submitted himself to the will of God with complete satisfaction.

Infinite resignation, however, is *not* the highest element in faith; for perfect faith calls for an action which involves the whole self. Still, resignation prepares for faith. "The infinite resignation is the last stage prior to faith, so that one who has not made this movement has not faith; for only in the infinite resignation do I become clear to myself with respect to my eternal validity, and only then can there be any question of grasping existence by virtue of faith."[11]

Some followers of God are offended by the link between faith and good works, but neither Abraham, James, nor Kierkegaard was. With this in view, then, the epistle of James becomes an "epistle of gold." Daily moral action, by which an existing individual makes it clear that he trusts the God whom he has not seen, not only opens the way for duty to be translated into valor, but the courage for such a translation comes from the Holy Spirit of God. Personal virtue — which connects directly with subjective truth as seen by Kierkegaard — is very necessary to the religious life. This is why Abraham enjoys such a high rank in the community of believers, Jewish or Gentile.

> Therefore, whereas the tragic hero is great by reason of his moral virtue, Abraham is great by reason of a personal virtue. In Abraham's life there is no higher expression for the ethical than this, that the father shall love his son. . . . Why then did Abraham do it [take steps to slay Isaac]? For God's sake, and (in complete identity with this) for his own sake. He did it for God's sake because God required this proof of his faith;

---

[10] *Ibid.*, p. 28.
[11] *Ibid.*, pp. 65-66.

for his own sake he did it in order that he might furnish the proof.[12]

Kierkegaard was not disturbed by the fact that Abraham, in his task of offering up Isaac, was not upset; for Kierkegaard was firmly persuaded that the task itself was a form of religious testing, and that Abraham willingly met the test with his whole being.

Whereas we tend to confine our view of temptation to seduction, Kierkegaard went on to speak of a certain kind of religious testing or *"Anfechtung."* He shifted the emphasis from temptation as seduction to temptation which brings the self up against something repulsive, or which may contain an element of danger — as illustrated by Christ's reference to temptation in the Lord's Prayer. In this Prayer the reference to temptation is a reference to testing. *"Anfechtung* is in the sphere of the God-relationship what temptation is in the ethical sphere."[13] The element of testing, which may take on the form of repulsion, traces to a conflict between the terms of ethical duty and the elements which form the will of God. "A temptation — but what does that mean? What ordinarily tempts a man is that which would keep him from doing his duty, but in this case [Abraham's] the temptation is itself the ethical . . . which would keep him from doing God's will."[14] Hence, the temptation of a religiously committed person (in addition to the attractions of pride, lust, etc.) is to become so devoted to the terms of ethical duty that a respect for the absoluteness of God's will is lost.

> In temptation, it is the lower that tempts, in *Anfechtung* it is the higher; in temptation, it is the lower that allures the individual, in *Anfechtung* it is the higher that, as if jealous of the individual, tries to frighten him back. *Anfechtung* therefore originates first in the essentially religious sphere, and occurs there only in the final stage, increasing quite properly in proportion to the intensity of the religiosity, because the individual has discovered the limit, and *Anfechtung* expresses the reaction of the limit against the finite individual. . . . *Anfechtung* is pre-

---

[12] *Ibid.,* pp. 88-89.
[13] Kierkgaard, *Concluding Unscientific Postscript,* p. 410.
[14] Kierkegaard, *Fear and Trembling,* p. 89.

cisely the reaction to the absolute expression for the absolute relationship. Temptation assails the individual in his weak moments, while *Anfechtung* is the nemesis upon the strong moment in the absolute relationship. Temptation therefore stands in connection with the individual's ethical habitus, while *Anfechtung* on the contrary is without continuity, and is the opposition of the absolute itself.[15]

It is within the context of this special reference to *Anfechtung* that we are to judge Kierkegaard's interpretation of Abraham's faith. When Abraham reached for the knife and was about to make a human sacrifice of his own son, Isaac, the ethical within him cried out for primary attention. If Abraham had given in to this cry of ethics, refusing to offer up his son, he would have become a victim of *Anfechtung*. Both Abraham and Kierkegaard admitted that the act of offering up Isaac, when judged by ethical standards, was plain murder. And yet, since Abraham was firmly persuaded that he was under a special divine command, he could only prove his faith by subordinating the criteria of ethics to the will of the absolute God. It was in this act of willingness to subordinate everything relative to the absolute — even the life of a child — that Abraham became a model of faith for believers in all generations. "The story of Abraham contains therefore a teleological suspension of the ethical."[16]

By now it is increasingly evident that ". . . faith is a passion."[17] The existing individual commits everything to the absoluteness of God. The more willing he is to trust all, the more consistent and fruitful his faith becomes. By basing his life solely on God, he no longer is a superficial subdivision of some universal or a mere number in a group.

---

[15] Kierkegaard, *Concluding Unscientific Postscript*, pp. 410-411.
[16] Kierkegaard, *Fear and Trembling*, p. 100. Christians must not be too shocked by this principle — "a teleological suspension of the ethical" — for the very principle, or one similar to it, was in force when Christ died on the cross. Still, it is disappointing that Kierkegaard did not make an effort to develop a more convincing apology for faith at this point; for apart from the illumination which comes from apologetics, how can a Christian answer an errorist who tries to justify his conduct as "a teleological suspension of the ethical?"
[17] *Idem*.

Since Kierkegaard was not particularly interested in developing a consistent system, it is not surprising that the philosophy of faith based on the account of Abraham, is not carried through elsewhere. In fact, the most oft-repeated philosophy of faith was based on the incarnation, *i.e.*, Christ as the absolute paradox. In this case faith was required because all possibility of satisfying the probing of reason was shattered. "The God-Man is the paradox, absolutely the paradox; hence it is quite clear that the understanding must come to a standstill before it."[18] Reinhold Niebuhr spells out this paradox in very clear language.

> All definitions of Christ which affirm both his divinity and humanity in the sense that they ascribe both finite and historically conditioned and eternal and unconditioned qualities to his nature must verge on logical nonsense. It is possible for a character, event, or fact of history to point symbolically beyond history and to become a source of disclosure of an eternal meaning, purpose and power which bears history. But it is not possible for any person to be historical and unconditioned at the same time.[19]

Whereas Niebuhr rejected the metaphysical incarnation on the grounds of its being an offense to reason, Kierkegaard rejoiced in the offense because it provided what he sincerely felt was a needed stimulus for faith. "For without risk there is no faith, and the greater the risk the greater the faith...."[20] When the existing individual is willing to launch on a course demanding the deepest of personal passion, he has faith — the opposite of both sin and objective certainty.

Once again the existential side of Socrates commended itself to Kierkegaard as a parallel to Christian faith. Just as Socrates embraced the concept of immortality by staking his whole life on it, and then living as though it were the most certain and important of all things with which the mind and heart can make contact, so the vital Christian existentially stakes all on God in Christ. "A man considers within himself whether Christ is everything to him, and then he says, on this I stake

---

[18] Kierkegaard, *Training in Christianity*, p. 85.
[19] Reinhold Niebuhr, *The Nature and Destiny of Man*, II, 61.
[20] Kierkegaard, *Concluding Unscientific Postscript*, p. 188.

everything."[21] There is no objective, rational route that one can take to Christ; for if there were, as Kierkegaard evaluated the matter, we would once again find ourselves in the company of immediacy. A leap of inner passion is *sine qua non* for genuine Christian faith. "I cannot acquire an immediate certainty as to whether I have faith — for to believe means precisely that dialectical hovering which, although in fear and trembling, never despairs; faith is an infinite self-made care as to whether one has faith — and that self-made care is faith."[22]

Absolute commitment to the will of God, which is only another way of expressing the substance of faith, must be the result of a despairing heart; it cannot be the result of a series of rationally persuasive arguments.

Although Kierkegaard concentrated on the incarnation as the absolute paradox, this does not mean that he paid no attention to other elements in the Christian religion which were apparently offensive to the understanding. His survey of nature, for example, left him with a measure of the same paradox which he felt was so prominent in the incarnation.

> I contemplate the order of nature in the hope of finding God, and I see omnipotence and wisdom; but I also see much else that disturbs my mind and excites anxiety. The sum of all this is an objective uncertainty. But it is for this very reason that the inwardness becomes as intense as it is, for it embraces this objective uncertainty with the entire passion of the infinite.[23]

Next, Kierkegaard confronted a severe paradox when he contemplated the nature of God. But if this paradox is as severe as it is here depicted, one wonders what meaning there is to speak of man as made in the image of God, or what prospect there is for Christian theology. But we had best let Kierkegaard speak at this point.

> For how should the Reason be able to understand what is absolutely different from itself? If this is not immediately evident, it will become clearer in the light of the consequences; for if God is absolutely unlike man, then man is absolutely unlike God;

---

21 Kierkegaard, *Journals*, 763.
22 *Idem*.
23 Kierkegaard, *Concluding Unscientific Postscript*, p. 182.

but how could the Reason be expected to understand this? Here we seem to be confronted with a paradox. Merely to obtain the knowledge that God is unlike him, man needs the help of God; and now he learns that God is absolutely different from himself. But if God and man are absolutely different, this cannot be accounted for on the basis of what man derives from God, for in so far they are akin.[24]

Each existing individual needs the promise of eternal life, but this promise can come only from God, the author of life. Thus, the important position held by faith; for faith reassures the existing individual that his life *is* held by God in Christ, and that consequently he is heir to eternal happiness.

B. *Suffering*

If a Christian looks to the writings of Kierkegaard for a defense of perpetual tranquility, he is wide of the mark. Aesthetic living may guarantee a measure of peace, though even this way of life is sullied by struggle and defeat. But the *religious* life, as Kierkegaard interpreted it, is characterized by inevitable suffering. The last stage in the religious life is that act of self-annihilation in which the ideal task of *being* an existing individual and the impossibility of fulfilling it concretely war against each other. The ideal task is to be like Jesus Christ: to mediate eternity (self-giving love) through passionate, moment-by-moment decisions in time. The ideal, on the one hand, and the existing individual's seeking to mediate the ideal, on the other, are so incompatibly related that perpetual tranquility in the religious life is ruled out *a priori*. An awareness of this incompatibility, together with a sensitivity to the fact that sin and guilt take up lodging in the heart, form the basic reasons for the inevitability of religious suffering. To deny the ideal is but a way of denying the Christian view of an existing individual; while to admit the ideal is to make suffering an expected part of religious experience. The apostle Paul set down a remarkable review of the inevitable spiritual suffering through which every Christian must pass.

---

[24] Kierkegaard, *Philosophical Fragments*, p. 37.

> We know that the law is spiritual; but I am carnal, sold under sin. I do not understand my own actions. For I do not do what I want, but I do the very thing I hate. Now if I do what I do not want, I agree that the law is good. So then it is no longer I that do it, but sin which dwells within me. For I know that nothing good dwells within me, that is, in my flesh. I can will what is right, but I cannot do it. For I do not do the good I want, but the evil I do not want is what I do. Now if I do what I do not want, it is no longer I that do it, but sin which dwells within me. So I find it to be a law that when I want to do right, evil lies close at hand. For I delight in the law of God, in my inmost self, but I see in my members another law at war with the law of my mind and making me captive to the law of sin which dwells in my members. Wretched man that I am! Who will deliver me from this body of death?[25]

Because religious suffering is inevitable, it serves as evidence to God and the existing individual that the self is aware of both its guilt and of its determination to come to grips with it. In grace God accepts suffering as a religious substitute for the ideal fulfillment of the law.

Suffering, it must be stressed, has religious meaning only when it is experienced in daily life. This removes the theoretical element; for a Christian must at one and the same time balance an absolute relationship to an absolute end, and a relative relationship to relative ends. As long as the terms of the religious life are objectively confined to paper, spiritual suffering will inevitably disappear. An existential union of ideal duty and concrete act is accomplished only when an absolute devotion to God is harmonized with a relative devotion to everything else. Thus, whenever the religious life is properly understood, suffering is an inevitability. The suffering is inner, of course, not physical. Physical suffering is contingent.

Because inner suffering is part of the religious life, it follows that immediacy, despite its provisional attraction, may never secure a lasting advantage. The aesthete lives for the moment. Blind to the absolute *telos* which accompanies the religious life, all he can do is to take in tidbits of empirical satisfaction which happen to appear along the way.

---

[25] Romans 7:14-24.

> *Immediacy is fortune,* for in the immediate consciousness there is no contradiction; the immediate individual is essentially seen as a fortunate individual, and *the view of life natural to immediacy* is one based on fortune. If one were to ask the immediate individual whence he has this view of life he would have to answer with virginal naïveté, "I do not myself understand it." The contradiction comes from without, and takes the form of misfortune. The immediate individual never comes to any understanding with misfortune, for he never becomes dialectical in himself; and if he does not manage to get rid of it, he finally reveals himself as lacking the poise to bear it. That is, he despairs, because he cannot grasp misfortune.[26]

There is suffering in immediacy, to be sure, but it is of a different kind than that of religious suffering. Immediacy suffers from a want of hope, for there is nothing in it beyond the moment. Immediacy puts no premium on faith in God; there is no genuine selfhood; there is no reason to expect eternal happiness after this brief life. The suffering of immediacy traces to the fact that the follower of the immediate devotes himself absolutely to relative ends.

Thus, there is inevitable suffering in *both* immediacy and the religious life, but immediacy looks to fortune, and thus is disappointed by suffering, while the religious life submits to the present incompatibility between the temporal and the eternal, thus making suffering an essential part of the Christian vocation. An existing individual simply does not exist unless he suffers — that is, he does not exist existentially and inwardly.

> The inwardness that is the core of the ethical and ethico-religious individual understands suffering ... as something essential. While the immediate individual involuntarily abstracts from misfortune, and fails to know that it is there as soon as it does not outwardly manifest itself, the religious individual has suffering constantly with him. He requires suffering in the same sense that the immediate individual requires fortune, and he requires and has suffering even in the absence of external misfortune; for it is not misfortune that he requires, in which case the relationship would be aesthetic, and he would remain essentially undialectical in himself.[27]

[26] Kierkegaard, *Concluding Unscientific Postscript,* p. 388.
[27] *Ibid.,* p. 389.

At first glance it may seem strange that inner suffering is a doorway to all the blessings which accompany the religious life, but suffering is an existential witness to the self's realization that it is bound by finitude, while God is absolute in his nature. *Perpetual* suffering shows that the self depends upon God at every moment for every gift which makes up life. "Immediacy expires in suffering; in suffering, religiosity begins to breathe."[28] The religious life needs no persuasion; it knows that in itself it is nothing.

Within these profound comments on suffering, however, Kierkegaard degraded the *poet* to a level that very few well-read people will accept. First, a renewed defense of religious suffering is made: "But suffering as the essential expression for existential pathos means that suffering is real, or that the reality of the suffering constitutes the existential pathos; and by *the reality of the suffering is meant its persistence as essential for the pathetic relationship to an eternal happiness.*"[29] Then comes the following: "Viewed religiously, it is necessary . . . to comprehend the suffering and to remain in it, so that the reflection is directed *upon* the suffering and not *away* from it."[30] Kierkegaard freely granted that the poet lives a life which seems to be religious, but which in fact is a façade because it is a qualitatively different life. The charge is made — quite without sufficient evidence — that the poet, with all his facility in the use of words, is basically an ignorant person, in particular when it comes to understanding and explaining suffering as an integral part of the existential life. "A poet is often a sufferer in existence, but what we reflect upon is the poetic productivity which is thereby brought about. The existing poet who suffers in his existence does not really comprehend his suffering, he does not penetrate more and more deeply into it, but in his suffering he seeks away from the suffering and finds ease in poetic production, in the poetic anticipation of a more perfect, i.e., a happier, order of things."[31] It is hard to explain how Kierke-

---

[28] *Ibid.*, p. 390.
[29] *Ibid.*, p. 396.
[30] *Ibid.*, p. 397.
[31] *Idem.*

gaard wandered into this field, for the more he indicted the poet, the more he exhibited his own prejudice.

> The poet can explain (transfigure) the whole of existence, but he cannot explain himself, because he will not become religious and so understand the secret of suffering as the form of the highest life, higher than all fortune and different from all misfortune. For herein lies the severity of the religious consciousness, that it begins by making everything more strict, and that it is not related to poesy as merely a new wishful invention, an entirely novel way of escape that poesy has not dreamed of, but as a difficulty which creates men in the same sense that war creates heroes.[32]

At this point it seems that Kierkegaard was relying on nothing less than philosophic imagination, for some of the greatest hymns of the church were written by poets who inwardly knew the meaning of religious suffering.

Because the suffering of the Christian is inevitable, and because both immanence and aestheticism rest in fortune, the suffering of the religious life is often branded as unadulterated foolishness. Hence, Kierkegaard wisely advised that it is wrong to make the world look pleasant and attractive to one who is thinking of becoming a Christian.

> We should truly hate to make a youth conceited, and early teach him to form the habit of judging the world; God forbid that any word of ours should be able to contribute to the development of such unsoundness in a man. We believe in making his inner life so strenuous that from the very beginning he learns to think otherwise, for it is certainly a perverted hatred of the world which, possibly without even having once considered the tremendous responsibility involved, wishes to be persecuted. But . . . we should truly hate to deceive a youth by keeping silent about the difficulty and keeping silent at the very moment when we are trying to recommend the Christian way of life, for then and just then is the time to speak. Confidently and fearlessly we dare to recommend the Christian way of life, and to add that its reward, to put it mildly, will be the ingratitude of the world. We regard it as our duty to say this *in time,* so that we may not sometimes recommend Christianity by omitting any of its essential difficulties, and at other times, perhaps because of some particular text, find some ground of comfort

[32] *Ibid.,* pp. 397-398.

for it in the life attempted. No, just at the time when the Christian way is being most strongly recommended, the difficulty must be simultaneously emphasized. It is unchristian sophistry if anyone reasons in this way: "Let us use every means to win men to the Christian way of life, and then when sometime adversities come upon them, then we shall have the remedy, then will be the time to speak about it." But this is the deception: that it might be possible for a Christian to escape these adversities, just as some people are fortunate in not being tried by poverty or sickness. That is, it places the opposition of the world in an accidental relation to the Christian way, not in an essential relation: opposition may perhaps come, but then again it may not. However, such a consideration is absolutely unchristian.[33]

The devotee of this world overlooks the paradoxical aspects of life; he fondly presumes that all will work out well in the end.

Because the true suffering of Christianity can be so easily imitated, it is necessary that we forthrightly expose such imitations. Suffering for the sake of Christ takes a toll on the *inner* man. All external suffering is sheer contingency. Because man is a synthesis of time and eternity, he is an existential person only when he dwells within a spiritual realization of this synthesis. There simply is no inner suffering until the self existentially grasps the essential contradiction which blankets existence itself. This means that genuine religious suffering is inward, essential, and perpetual. Any species of suffering which falls short of these conditions falls short of Christianity itself.

Aesthetic suffering, for example, seems to be identical with religious suffering, but the similarity is fraudulent in its very essence.

> The reality of the suffering signifies its essential persistence, and is its essential relation to the religious life. Aesthetically, suffering stands in an accidental relation to existence. Such accidental suffering may indeed persist, but the persistence of that which is in itself accidental is not an essential persistence.[34]

A person may suffer for the sake of art or music with inwardness and intimacy, but this merely illustrates the accidental element in aesthetic suffering. Only Christianity unites essential suf-

---
[33] Kierkegaard, *Works of Love*, pp. 156-157.
[34] Kierkegaard, *Concluding Unscientific Postscript*, p. 398.

fering with a transforming hope, and it succeeds because it looks to an intimate tie between God and the contrite heart which is *permanent* — that is, which guarantees eternal happiness to the contrite heart.

> When the Scriptures say that God dwells in a contrite heart, this does not represent a transitory or momentary relationship (in that case the use of the word "dwell" would be extremely unfortunate), but expresses on the contrary the essential significance of suffering for the God-relationship.[35]

Self-flagellation effectively illustrates a form of religious suffering. But once again we are not dealing with Christian terms. The person who tortures himself to gain the pleasure of God is a fool; for instead of confessing himself to be nothing in himself, he thinks of self-flagellation as an expedient which God ought to respect. The suffering of self-inflicted torture is a *quantitative* determinant, while inner, Christian suffering is a *qualitative* determinant. These are harsh but inescapable alternatives. The person who endures religious suffering in Christianity realizes that his very life — moment-by-moment — is part of an essential contradiction, the contradiction of having to meet the terms of an absolute *telos* with relative means. But the zealot of self-flagellation not only nurses the notion that by his acts of torture he will dissolve life's contradictions, but he also rejects the absolute in favor of the relative. Although he is a devout advocate of contingency, he imagines that he is so congenially related to the higher powers of the universe that by his acts of self-torture he can easily meet all that is required of him. His satisfaction with contingency merely shows his distance from essential expressions of suffering, and thus from the thesis, "Truth is subjectivity." "The religious individual sustains a relationship to an eternal happiness, and the sign of this relationship is suffering, and suffering is its essential expression — for an existing individual."[36]

A martyr may be named by many as the one who most perfectly illustrates inner suffering. Since he is ready to lay down

---

[35] *Ibid.*, p. 399.
[36] *Ibid.*, p. 407.

his life, what more could be asked of him? In the act of martyrdom, however, physical suffering does not prove the presence of inner suffering until special conditions are met. "... if I deliver my body to be burned, but have not love, I gain nothing."[37] Whenever death is linked with fortune — and suicide is a kind of fortune — we immediately return to the aesthetic fallacy. This means that even suffering unto death is not, in and of itself, necessarily evidence of true, inner suffering. Becoming a martyr may only serve as a convenient way of avoiding the ethical responsibility of being an existing individual.

> No, when the individual is secure in his God-relationship and suffers only outwardly, then this is not religious suffering. Such suffering is subject to an aesthetic dialectic, like misfortune to the immediate consciousness; it may be present and it may be absent. But no one is justified in denying that a human being is religious because no blow of misfortune fell upon him. But because he is without experience of such misfortune he is not on that account without suffering, if in fact he is religious; for suffering is precisely the expression for the God-relationship, that is, the religious suffering, which signalizes the God-relationship and the fact that the individual has not arrived at happiness by emancipating himself from a religious relationship to an absolute *telos*.[38]

If relative factors could serve as well as absolute factors, then there is no doubt that the martyr would enjoy an advantage which is denied others. In this case we would not only face the paradox that it is better to die than to live; but, more seriously, the absolute would be withdrawn from the religious scene. Certainly this is one of the main reasons why Christianity teaches that God judges the *heart* of the believer, thus restoring the element of absoluteness.

The suffering of fatalism is perhaps the most convincing alternative to the truth; for whether we care for it or not, the significance of life is *connected* with sorrow. Fatalism manages to preserve its position by its association with necessity and perpetuity. Under the pressure of fatalism the existing individual is made part and parcel of the world process. Out

---

[37] I Corinthians 13:3.
[38] Kierkegaard, *Concluding Unscientific Postscript*, p. 405.

of this crucifixion of personal freedom comes the suffering of resignation. Such a suffering is not connected with either a spiritual awareness of God or the need for repentance; hence, the *necessity* of the suffering — in whatever degree or amount it happens to exist — is not inward in the strict sense of the term. There is an element of paradox in fatalism, to be sure, but it reflects the outward, not the inward. Since the fatalist believes that he could avoid suffering under ideal conditions, his suffering is neither spiritual nor essential. Fatalism is, at best, a sorrow of this world. Until an existential choice of the self is made, distress will result.

> But when one chooses oneself abstractly one does not choose oneself ethically. Only when in his choice a man has assumed himself, is clad in himself, has so totally penetrated himself that every movement is attended by the consciousness of a responsibility for himself, only then has he chosen himself ethically, only then has he repented himself, only then is he concrete, only then is he in his total isolation in absolute continuity with the reality to which he belongs.[39]

Since there is a contradictory element in religious suffering, suffering and humor have something in common. In a way it is humorous to realize that a deeply religious man, while maintaining a strict devotion to God, outwardly looks like all other men. Although the condition of his heart is fully known to God, it is hidden from those about him.

Because of his appreciation for the contradictory elements in life, the humorist is not far from the kingdom. "Since an existing humorist presents the closest approximation to the religious, he has also an essential conception of the suffering in which life is involved, in that he does not apprehend existence as one thing, and fortune or misfortune as something happening to the existing individual, but exists so that suffering is for him relevant to existence."[40]

Unlike the aesthete, the cautious humorist does not superficially assign suffering to a contingent place which fortunate circumstances can overcome. He frankly acknowledges that

---

[39] Kierkegaard, *Either/Or*, II, 208.
[40] Kierkegaard, *Concluding Unscientific Postscript*, p. 400.

suffering and existence are bound together. In this strange way it is safe to say that religious suffering and comical suffering have much in common, for ". . . it is true without exception that the more thoroughly and substantially a human being exists, the more he will discover the comical."[41]

The similarity ends, however, the moment the humorist is asked to *explain* the reason why suffering and existence go together. The humorist can smile as he passes through suffering, but he remains blind to the tie with God which makes religious suffering a proof of faith.

> . . . at that point the humorist turns deceptively aside and revokes the suffering in the form of the jest. He comprehends the significance of suffering as relevant to existence, but he does not comprehend the significance of the suffering itself; he understands that it belongs to existence, but does not understand its significance except through the principle that suffering belongs. The first thought is the pain in the humoristic consciousness, the second is the jest, and hence it comes about that one is tempted both to weep and to laugh when the humorist speaks. He touches upon the secret of existence in the pain, but then he goes home again.[42]

All the humorist can do is to smile at life, including its suffering. Therefore, if a spiritually disturbed individual goes to him for help, he receives no more than a jest.

> As a humorist exists, he also expresses himself; and in life one may sometimes hear a humorist speak, in books his remarks are most frequently distorted. Now let a humorist express himself, and he will speak for example as follows: "What is the meaning of life? Aye, tell me that; how should I know, we are born yesterday and know nothing. But one thing I do know, namely, that it is most comfortable to stride unknown through the world. . . ."[43]

Those who are accustomed to drawing hasty conclusions might suppose that religious suffering is the most comical of all situations. "The law for the comical is quite simple: it exists wherever there is contradiction. . . ."[44] Thus it would seem that

---

[41] *Ibid.*, p. 413.
[42] *Ibid.*, p. 400.
[43] *Ibid.*, p. 402.
[44] *Ibid.*, p. 466.

the greater the contradiction becomes, the greater the comedy becomes. But what could contain greater elements of contradiction than the fact that the Christian does not truly become an existing individual until he mediates eternity in time? The first part of the contradiction is this: that the person who already *is* must *become*. The second part is this: that eternity and time — whose union formed the absolute paradox in Jesus Christ — cannot be effectively mediated by creatures of guilt and dust. Kierkegaard forthrightly acknowledged the contradictory elements in the Christian faith, but he swiftly denied that there is anything comical about this faith.

> The matter is quite simple. The comical is present in every stage of life (only that the relative positions are different), for wherever there is life, there is contradiction, and wherever there is contradiction, the comical is present. The tragic and the comic are the same, in so far as both are based on contradiction; but *the tragic is the suffering contradiction, the comical, the painless contradiction.*[45]

Rather than sitting back and *smiling* about the mystery in which one is immersed by reason of life's contradictions, a conscientious Christian will *repent;* for he realizes that his life is nothing without God; but he also realizes that he does not consistently live by the concept of total dependence upon God. Unlike the aesthete, he cannot base hope on fortune; and unlike the fatalist, he cannot dismiss the question of personal responsibility because of universal determinism. Unless he comes to terms with his guilt, he fails to come to terms with himself. "To suffer for the doctrine, to *will* to suffer for the doctrine, not incidentally to suffer for it by chance — well, that kind of Christianity has gone out of use."[46]

A superficial reader might charge that suffering in Christianity brings more harm than it does good. At the sound of this objection Kierkegaard swiftly rose to speak. A religion without suffering might appeal to a man of this world, but the Christian realizes that it is impossible to accept the self and to live with a spiritual eye toward the eternal without suffering. Clever

---
[45] *Ibid.,* p. 459.
[46] Kierkegaard, *For Self-Examination and Judge for Yourselves!,* p. 209.

pates try to make life easier, but Kierkegaard was convinced that an existing individual has surrendered his dignity unless he strives at all times to live before God as a morally responsible person. Precious reward immediately follows; for when the disciple of Jesus Christ submits to the inevitability of religious suffering, he experiences a wonderful relief from earthly despair. In deciding *for* Christianity, rather than *against* it, a true calculus of values is kept in proper proportion. Since death will soon and inevitably overtake each of us, only a fool would live as if there is no need to dwell under the shadow of the Almighty. Unless we are in fellowship with God — and this calls for the suffering of ethical striving — how else will we gain the hope of eternal life (happiness)?

> In the finite sense there is nothing whatever to gain, and everything to lose. In the life of time the *expectation* of an eternal happiness is the highest reward, because an eternal happiness is the highest *telos;* and it is precisely a sign of the relationship to the absolute that there is not only no reward to expect, but suffering to bear. When the individual is no longer content with this, it means that he relapses into worldly wisdom. . . .[47]

The presence of suffering is no mark against Christianity, therefore, because *all* attempts to explain the significance of life, especially when the question of eternal life is faced, are plagued by suffering. "It is precisely here that the difficulty of sustaining an absolute relationship to an absolute *telos* manifests itself. Again and again men begin to look around for excuses, hoping to find some way of escape from thus having to walk on their toes, some way of evading — the relationship to the absolute."[48] Again, ". . . the absolute *telos* exists for the individual only when he yields it an absolute devotion. And since an eternal happiness is a *telos* for existing individuals, these two (the absolute end and the existing individual) cannot be conceived as realizing a union in existence in terms of rest."[49]

If minor misfortunes do not disturb an aesthete, the major

---

[47] Kierkegaard, *Concluding Unscientific Postscript*, p. 360.
[48] *Ibid.,* pp. 360-361.
[49] *Ibid.,* p. 355.

misfortune of physical death surely will. Since physical death is inevitable — thus establishing the universal question of whether or not we shall enjoy personal existence beyond the grave — the suffering of the aesthete is a genuine tragedy, for the consistent aesthete realizes that he is a misfit. Man is formed of such a delicate balance between temporal limitations and eternal potencies that it is impossible for him to think that he is nothing but an upright animal. The human spirit is endowed with an appetite for eternity. "That which really makes a man despair is not misfortune, but it is the fact that he lacks the eternal; despair is to lack the eternal; despair consists in not having undergone the change of eternity by duty's 'shalt.' "[50]

The suffering which grows out of a fear that death fathers non-being, is so great at times that relief is sought in idolatry. This supports the Augustinian conviction — which Kierkegaard wholeheartedly accepted — that man was made unto God, and he will not rest until he rests in God. An idolater tries to appease his need by constructing his own deity. The prophet Isaiah described such an effort as follows:

> He cuts down cedars; or he chooses a holm tree or an oak and lets it grow strong among the trees of the forest; he plants a cedar and the rain nourishes it. Then it becomes fuel for a man; he takes a part of it and warms himself, he kindles a fire and bakes bread; also he makes a god and worships it, he makes it a graven image and falls down before it. Half of it he burns in the fire; over the half he eats flesh, he roasts meat and is satisfied; also he warms himself and says, "Aha, I am warm, I have seen the fire!" And the rest of it he makes into a god, his idol; and falls down to it and worships it; he prays to it and says, "Deliver me, for thou art my god!"[51]

Both the Christian and the idolater suffer, to be sure, for the entire human race is doomed to pass through some kind of suffering. But the Christian's existential grasp of guilt provides him with such a reverent understanding of God that he is not betrayed into the cardinal sin of idolatry. He not only has a

---

[50] Kierkegaard, *Works of Love*, p. 34.
[51] Isaiah 44:14-17.

reasonable grasp of why suffering is inevitable in the religious life, but he is content to be man and not God — that is, if he is a *mature* Christian.

Although suffering is one of the chief ingredients of inwardness, this does not mean that peace of heart cannot be enjoyed during this earthly walk. On the contrary, the very inevitability of suffering *is* a cause for peace. In the last analysis we suffer because God is God. Our relation to God carries moral responsibility; and this relation, if it is viewed with the moment-by-moment seriousness that it deserves, is as perpetual as it is demanding. Hence, the task of being an individual and a Christian is very, very difficult, for the absolute nature of ethics illuminates the absoluteness of the divine nature. Still, the Christian who knows the reason *why* he suffers, is a person who derives peace from the very fact that he suffers.

> The exercise of the absolute distinction makes life absolutely strenuous, precisely when the individual remains in the finite and simultaneously maintains an absolute relationship to the absolute *telos* and a relative relationship to the relative. But in this strenuous exertion there is nevertheless a tranquillity and a peace; for absolutely, or with all one's strength, and with the renunciation of everything else, to maintain a relationship to the absolute *telos* is no contradiction, but is the absolute correspondence of like to like. The tortured self-contradiction of worldly passion arises from the attempt to sustain an *absolute* relationship to a relative *telos*. Avarice, vanity, envy, and so forth, are thus essentially forms of madness; for it is precisely the most general expression for madness that the individual has an absolute relationship to what is relative.[52]

C. *Hope*

As we now turn our attention to hope as one of the four important conditions of inwardness, it is necessary to point out that Kierkegaard interpreted the meaning of hope from two different perspectives. We shall concentrate for the most part on the view developed in *Works of Love*, in the chapter entitled, "Love Hopeth All Things — and Yet Is Never Put to Shame." This view is as skillfully written as it is biblically accurate.

[52] Kierkegaard, *Concluding Unscientific Postscript*, pp. 377-378.

It so happens, however, that in the first volume of *Either/Or*, a book written several years before *Works of Love*, Kierkegaard took a very disparaging view of hope. When a man hopes, misery results; for man's capacity to hope is wretched at its best.

> When this happens, it is . . . due to the fact that he constantly hopes something that should be remembered; his hope constantly disappoints him, and in disappointing him, reveals to him that it is not because the realization of his hope is postponed, but because it is already past and gone, has already been experienced, or should have been experienced, and thus has passed over into memory . . . . it is due to the fact that he always remembers that for which he ought to hope; for the future he has already anticipated in thought, in thought already experienced it, and this experience he now remembers, instead of hoping for it. Consequently, what he hopes for lies behind him, what he remembers lies before him.[53]

In *Works of Love* Kierkegaard likened hope to a gust of fresh mountain breeze that floods a room which is corrupted with impure air. The impure air in this case is the corruption of aesthetic worldliness and immanence, and the refreshment is hope. When purpose and direction in life seem to be lost, hope comes to the rescue; it revives the depressed individual by seizing eternity as a *possibility*. "Christianity's hope is eternity; and Christ is the Way; His abasement is the Way, but also when He ascends into heaven He would also be the Way."[54]

Kierkegaard's mature view of hope can best be understood and appreciated by glancing at his anthropology. Man, a synthesis of time and eternity, is a creature whose individuality remains unaccented until he passionately strives to mediate eternity in time. We find at once, however, that paradox limits the understanding; for man *cannot*, with all his efforts, mediate the eternal in time. It turns out, therefore, that paradox stimulates repentance, self-denial, and hope. Hope, by reaching out its spiritual arms, seizes eternity for the Christian believer, though not as an existential possession (for paradox forbids such possession), but as a passionate possibility instead.

[53] Kierkegaard, *Either/Or*, I, 184.
[54] Kierkegaard, *Works of Love*, p. 200.

Hope accepts as an earnest what absolute existential living demands as fulfillment.

> For hoping means the synthesis of the eternal and the temporal; the consequence is that the expression for the task of hope in the form of eternity is to hope all things; for the task of hope in the form of the temporal existence always to hope. One expression is no truer than the other; on the contrary, each of the expressions becomes untrue if it is set in opposition to the other, instead of being united in expressing the same thing: at every moment always to hope all things.[55]

There are at least three complementary reasons why the eternal cannot become an existential part of the finite creation. *First*, the eternal cannot become the present, for the present is a series of contingencies which separate the eternity of the past from the eternity of the future. Before the present can even be reviewed, it has already become part of the past. *Second*, the eternal cannot become the past, for the past is nothing but a series of possibilities which have become actual. The eternal is the necessary; it cannot be displaced by possibilities. Jehovah is the eternal I Am. *Third*, the eternal cannot become the future, for the future is also nothing but a varied assembly of possibilities: possibilities which may become, and which may not become. Therefore, Kierkegaard saw no other way in which the eternal could enter time than through hope. By means of hope, we repeat, the spiritual faculties of man seize eternity as a possibility.

Since Kierkegaard associated hope with possibility, it would seem that hope has nothing to do with reality. This does not follow, for hope's hold on possibility is also a hold on reality — reality as conceived by faith and not by worldly wisdom, of course. Hence, this particular kind of reality is not something which can be set up for public display; rather, it is that which the hands of hope seize, as the free, existing individual faces eternity.

> To lay hold expectantly on the possibility of the good is *to hope*, which just for this reason cannot be any temporal expectation, but is an eternal hope. To lay hold expectantly on the pos-

[55] *Ibid.*, p. 201.

sibility of evil is *to fear*. But the one who hopes as well as the one who fears is expectant. Yet as soon as the choice is made, the possible is changed, for the possibility of the good is the eternal. It is only in the moment of contact that the doubleness of the possible is equal. By the decision to choose hope one decides, therefore, infinitely more than it seems, for it is an eternal decision. Only in the mere possibility, hence for the merely or indifferently expectant, are the possibilities of good and evil equal; in the making of a distinction (and choice is the making of a distinction) is the possibility of the good more than possibility, for it is the eternal. Hence it happens that he who hopes can never be deceived; for to hope is to expect the possibility of the good, but the possibility of good is the eternal.[56]

Since the essence of hope may be corrupted so easily, we must cautiously distinguish it from the sort of frivolous yearnings which are so characteristic of a child who hopes for more candy, more toys, and more money. "Still, if one hopes for something for which it is a disgrace to hope, regardless of whether the hope is fulfilled or not, one does not really hope. It is a misuse of the noble word 'hope' to juxtapose it with anything like that; for the fact of hoping lays hold essentially and eternally on the good — so one can never be disgraced by hoping."[57] The element of truth in childish hope is this: that it is inspired by a zeal to possess that which is just out of reach. The element of error in childish hope is this: that the zeal is not based on an appreciation of the essential predicament of man.

Religious hope is never the solitary possession of any single group, for hope is the standing means by which eternity is spiritually united with the affairs of the temporal order.

> One thinks to speak empirically by dividing a man's life into certain periods and years, and then calling the first period that of hope or of possibility. What nonsense! In that way one absolutely leaves out the eternal in speaking about hope, and yet one talks about hope. But how is that possible, since hope lays hold on the possibility of the good, and thereby on the eternal! On the other hand, how is it possible to speak about hope in such a way that one must assume that it belongs ex-

[56] *Ibid.*, p. 202.
[57] *Ibid.*, p. 211.

clusively to a certain age? The eternal certainly extends over the whole life, so there is and consequently must be hope until the last, so there is consequently no exclusive age which is hope's, but the whole of one's life must be the time of hope![58]

The blessing of hope is preserved for all Christians by the happy prospect that the essential nature of the human species does not change. Spirit, which is the faculty of freedom in the inner man, can only be gratified by a possession of the eternal; and the only way that the eternal can be made a present possession is by the spiritual exercise of hope. A person who refuses to stand tall and hope is, before God, an incomplete person; for to be lacking in hope is the same as to be lacking in spirit.

This means that hope takes hold of the individual who believes he will become nothing apart from a personal possession of the eternal. Hope does not solve this form of anxiety by converting eternity into an actual empirical entity. Rather, it teaches a man of faith how to lay hold of eternity as a possibility.

It is only because eternity may become a spiritual possibility (through the exercise of hope), that the disturbed individual finds relief.

> If eternity were sometime and in its own language to set man the task without regard for its apprehension and his limited ability: the man would be in despair. But then it is truly wonderful that this, the greatest power, eternity, can make itself so small, that it is so divisible, that that which is everlastingly one, by putting on the form of the future, of the possible, by the help of hope, educates the child of the temporal existence (the man), teaches him to hope (for hoping is itself an education, is the laying hold on the eternal), if he does not then voluntarily austerely choose to be dispirited through fear, or if he does not impudently choose to despair, that is, to evade the education of the possibility. Rightly understood, the eternal assigns only a little portion at a time in the possibility. Eternity is through the possible always *near* enough at hand, and yet *far* enough away to keep a man moving forward, progressing, toward the eternal. Thus eternity draws and lures man by the possibility from the cradle to the grave, if he will but choose to hope.[59]

[58] *Ibid.,* p. 203.
[59] *Ibid.,* p. 204.

The enemy of hope is fear, for fear is a shrinking of spirit (caught in the dizziness of freedom) from pressing on to the full heights of possibility. Fear cringes from reaching out to the eternal as possibility, preferring instead the withdrawal of despair.

> Hope does not lie as a matter of course in the possibility, for fear may also lie in it. But the one who chooses hope, him the possibility, by the aid of hope, teaches to hope. Still the possibility of fear, the severity, remains, secretly present as a possibility, if it should be needed for the sake of education, for the purpose of arousing; but it remains hidden, while the eternal allures by the aid of hope. For the alluring always consists in being equally as *near* as *far away*, whereby the hopeful one is always kept hoping, hoping everything, preserved in hope for the eternal, which in the temporal existence is the possible.[60]

While both faith and despair know the good, faith alone presses on to hope. Thus, an ignorance of what is required of one is *not* the crux of the problem. "The despairing one *knows,* too, what lies in the possibility, and yet he gives up the possibility (for renouncing the possibility is just what despair means), or, even more correctly, he ventures impudently to *assume* the impossibility of the good."[61]

The devout follower of this world, although blinded to the comfort which hope brings the dedicated Christian, believes he has an advantage over those who look to eternity. And indeed the surface advantage which he enjoys *is* superficially attractive. "Acting cleverly is, namely, incompleteness, whereby one undeniably gets farthest in the world, gains worldly goods and advantages, and the world's honor, because the world and worldly advantages are, everlastingly understood, incompleteness. But neither eternity nor the Holy Scriptures have ever taught any man to strive to come far or farthest in the world; on the contrary they warn him not to come too far in the world, in order, if possible, to keep himself pure from the world's pollution."[62]

Hope is listed among the conditions of inwardness because it

[60] *Idem.*
[61] *Ibid.,* p. 205.
[62] *Ibid.,* p. 211.

is a release from the suffering brought on by an existential effort to complete the self ethically through a mediation of the eternal in time. Hope helps one rejoice in the spiritual conviction that a dimension of being transcends the temporal. The more one stresses the ethical, the existential, and the religious, the more necessary hope becomes; for the self realizes to a degree previously hidden that the self *cannot* attain perfection this side of eternity. Thus, hope is an antidote for skepticism.

D. *Love*

When it comes to it, Kierkegaard realized that love is the richest, the most important condition of inwardness. Whereas hope is concealed in the heart, love is both inward and outward. Moreover, love plays a chief role in making the existing individual the true point of union between the temporal and the eternal. "What is it which connects the temporal and the eternal, what except love, which just for this reason is before everything, and which abides when everything else is past?"[63] Because of its very nature, love is the strongest stimulus to the self-giving capacities in man. Love confronts man with an eternal task. Although human nature is limited by time, space, and knowledge, it suffers no limits from love. Even if love *should* reach ideal temporal heights, it would still have all eternity to reach even higher.

Love cannot be stored up, like insect specimens or jars of water. Love is vitally related to the individual, for the individual remains only a spiritual potentiality until his capacity for love is released. This means that the thesis, "Truth is subjectivity," is but another way of stating the Christian conviction that truth is love, and that the ethical manners of the living person give reality to the substance of love. Therefore, whenever a person turns from the task of love, he actually turns from himself. He gives up individual existence — spiritually and existentially understood. He may continue to occupy

[63] *Ibid.*, p. 6.

space, to be sure; but this is nothing of which to boast, for corpses *also* continue to occupy space.

> To defraud oneself of love is the most terrible deception of all. It is an eternal loss for which there is no compensation either here or in eternity. . . . Much has also been said about being deceived by life or in life; but one who, self-deceived, defrauded himself of living, has suffered an irreparable loss . . . . the self-deceived has prevented himself from gaining the eternal. Oh, what has one whose love made him a victim of human deception really lost if in eternity it appears that love abides while the deception has ceased![64]

Much could be said about the nature of Christian love, but two elements make this love unique.

First, Christian love is unique because *God* is love in his very essence. The prayer of Kierkegaard, which begins *Works of Love,* is (despite its length) perhaps the richest treatment of this first element in the whole of Kierkegaard's writings.

> How could anything rightly be said about love if Thou wert forgotten, Thou God of Love, from whom all love comes in heaven and on earth; Thou who didst hold nothing back but didst give everything in love; Thou who art love, so the lover is only what he is through being in Thee! How could anything rightly be said about love if Thou wert forgotten, Thou who didst make manifest what love is, Thou, our Saviour and Redeemer, who gave Himself to save us all! How could anything rightly be said about love if Thou wert forgotten, Thou Spirit of Love, Thou who dost abate nothing of Thine own, but dost call to mind that sacrifice of love, dost remind the believer to love as he is loved, and his neighbor as himself! O Eternal Love! Thou who art everywhere present, and never without testimony in what may here be said about love, or about works of love. For it is certainly true that there are some acts which the human language particularly and narrow-mindedly calls acts of charity; but in heaven it is certainly true that no act can be pleasing unless it is an act of love: sincere in its self-abnegation, a necessity for love, and, just because of this, without claim or merit.[65]

Second, Christian love is unique because it introduces *self-love*

---

[64] *Ibid.,* p. 5.
[65] *Ibid.,* p. 4.

as the normative measure of love for others. In one stroke biblical ethics defines what is doubtless man's most demanding horizontal, moral obligation. A believer is commanded to love his neighbor, not in a wonderful or sacrificial way, but *as himself*.

> If the commandment about loving one's neighbor were expressed in some other way than by the use of this little phrase, 'as thyself,' which is at once so easy to use and yet has the tension of eternity, then the commandment would not be able thus to master the self-love. . . . Long and shrewd speeches might be made about how a man ought to love his neighbor; and then, after all the speeches had been heard, self-love could still hit upon an excuse and find a way of escape, because the subject had not been absolutely exhausted; all alternatives had not been canvassed; because something had been forgotten, or not accurately and bindingly enough expressed and described.[66]

The criterion of self-love imposes infinite conditions upon the ethical life; for whenever a person attempts to find out how much he loves himself, he is lost for an answer. Today's self-love, being compounded with the most vital self-interest, surpasses yesterday's self-love and that of the many days before yesterday. This means that a possibility/impossibility dialectic — an ethical commentary upon the central existential thesis, "Truth is subjectivity" — is created. "Certainly no wrestler can get so tight a clinch upon his opponent as that with which this commandment embraces the selfishness which cannot stir from its place."[67] Such adverbs as "greatly," "strenuously," or "persistently" lack the eternal element contained in self-love as a measure of horizontal love, that is, love to others about us.

Fundamental to all, of course, is the *vertical* direction of love, the love which we properly return to God for the single yet sufficient reason that he is God. The criterion of love in this case is fixed by the majesty and holiness of him who is being loved.

> There is only One whom a man may with the truth of the eternal love better than himself, that is God. Therefore it does not say, "Thou shalt love God as thyself," but it says, "Thou

[66] *Ibid.*, p. 15.
[67] *Idem.*

shalt love the Lord thy God with all thy heart and with all thy soul and with all thy mind." A man must love God in unconditional *obedience* and love Him in *adoration*. It would be ungodliness if any man dared to love himself in this way, or dared to love another man in this way, or dared to permit another man to love him in this way. . . . God you must love in unconditional obedience even if that which He demands of you may seem injurious to you, moreover injurious to His own interests.[68]

The horizontal and vertical obligations so exhaust man's daily, existential responsibilities that no conceivable limit can be placed on the outreach of ethical freedom. In the act of love, however, man is not *essentially* an existing individual, for he is only *contingently* existential what God is existential *in se*. As we have noted at another point, "God is love, therefore we can resemble God only in loving. . . ."[69]

It is this ethical possibility/impossibility dialectic which accounts for the inevitability of both hope and suffering in the Christian religion. Since a Christian is commanded to *do* what he *cannot* do, the ethical ideal is at once a possibility and an impossibility. Out of the possibility rises hope, while out of the impossibility comes suffering. Love is assigned to man, not as a comfortable suggestion which may or may not be followed, depending upon the mood that man happens to be in at the time. Rather, it is a divine command. When conscience is strictly associated with a failure to carry out the terms of love, it is eternity invading time. "*Only when it is a duty to love, only then is love everlastingly secure against every change; everlastingly emancipated in blessed independence; everlastingly happy, assured against despair.*"[70]

It may seem that insufficient space has been given to the vertical duty of love. Perhaps so. But no defense of the chapter at this point will be attempted. Let it be borne in mind at all times that we are trying to tell what *Kierkegaard* said, rather than to give our own opinions — here or elsewhere.

A Christian is to receive a neighbor just as he is, no matter

---

[68] *Ibid.*, p. 17.
[69] *Ibid.*, p. 52.
[70] *Ibid.*, p. 25.

how strange or revolting that neighbor may be. "When it is a duty in loving to love the men we see, *then it is important that in loving the individual, actual man, we do not slip in an imagined conception of how we believe or might wish that this man should be.* He who allows himself to do this does not love the man he sees, but again something unseen, his own idea, or something like it."[71] Thus, "Christ's love for Peter was . . . boundless; in loving Peter He perfected the task of loving the man one sees. He did not say: 'Peter must first be changed and become another man before I can love him.' No, exactly the converse. He said: 'Peter is Peter, and I love him. . . .' "[72]

Kierkegaard is very emphatic at this point; and since he is not disturbed by repetition, neither should we be. "Equality precisely consists in not making distinctions, and eternal equality is unconditionally not to make the least distinction, unqualifiedly not to make the least distinction; partiality, on the other hand, consists in making a distinction, a passionate distinction, in making an unlimited distinction."[73]

> The neighbor is your equal. The neighbor is not your beloved for whom you have a passionate partiality, not your friend for whom you have a passionate partiality. Nor, if you are an educated man, is your neighbor the one who is educated, with whom you are equal in education — for with your neighbor you have human equality before God. Nor is the neighbor the one who is more distinguished than yourself, that is, he is not your neighbor just because he is more distinguished than yourself, for loving him because he is more distinguished can then easily become partiality, and insofar selfishness. Nor is your neighbor one who is inferior to you, that is, insofar as he is humbler than yourself he is not your neighbor, for to love one because he is inferior to yourself can readily become the condescension of partiality, and insofar selfishness. No, loving your neighbor is a matter of equality.[74]

It may be easier to love those who love in return, but eternity places no premium on comfortable reciprocations of love. Hu-

[71] *Ibid.*, p. 133.
[72] *Ibid.*, p. 139.
[73] *Ibid.*, p. 48.
[74] *Ibid.*, p. 50.

man beings have inherent worth because they are made in the image of God, and for no other reason. Duty accompanies worth.

The student of this world is convinced that the most important step in making universal love is to improve social conditions. When all men share their goods equally, then they will love equally. But the dedicated Christian, who knows that eternity equalizes men, classifies this pagan scheme as another form of sin. It is not necessary to socialize men to equalize them morally, for they were made in the image of God from the beginning. "Christianity always allows the differences of the earthly life to persist, but this equality in rising above earthly differences is implicit in the commandment of love, in the loving one's neighbor."[75] The distinctions between men, when judged by Christian criteria, are insignificant. Therefore, all distinctions are "to hang loosely about the individual, loosely, like the cape the king casts off to reveal himself; loosely, like the ragged cloak in which a supernatural being has concealed itself."[76]

Now that we are coming near the end of our survey of the elements which make up the affirmative attributes of subjective truth, we may touch on the most relevant reason why Kierkegaard is simultaneously a stimulating and frustrating writer about the Christian religion. The reason is this: judged by spiritual and existential criteria, every living Christian is at best only *partly* a real individual. Since the final test of personal reality is self-giving love, it can be said that all Christians, whenever they are genuinely honest with themselves, will openly acknowledge that their lives fall short of ideal reality. Not only are their inner affections corrupted by excessive self-interest, but at times even resentment and hatred — or far worse things — are resorted to. It is obvious, therefore, that any peace in the Christian life traces to God's gift of grace, and not to achievements of rewardable righteousness in the self.

With this philosophy of personal reality briefly set before us,

[75] *Ibid.*, p. 60.
[76] *Ibid.*, p. 72.

we can appreciate the basic reason why Jesus Christ is the only complete individual. *Viewed from eternity,* of course, all who repent of their sins, and who strive to love as they should, are complete individuals. But under the conditions of sin and time, no one but Jesus Christ is a complete individual; for he alone, of all the men who walked this pilgrim path, met the absolute terms of the law of love at every moment in his life. Kierkegaard summarized this in the following way:

> Christ became the destruction of the law, because He was what it demanded, its destruction, its end; for when the demand is fulfilled, the demand exists only in the fulfillment, but hence it no longer exists anywhere as demand. . . . Moreover, He [Christ] was love, and His love was the fulness of the law. "No one could convict Him of any sin," not even the law which knows every conscience; "there was no deceit in His mouth," but everything in Him was truth; there was in His love not the hairsbreadth of a moment, of an emotion, of an interval between His purpose and the demand of the law for its fulfillment. He did not say "no," like that one brother, or "yes" like the other brother, for His meat was to do His Father's will; thus He was one with the Father, one with every demand of the law, so its perfecting was a necessity to Him, His sole need in life. The love in Him was perpetually active; there was no moment, not one single instant in His whole life when His love was merely a passive feeling which seeks expression while it lets time pass; or a mood which produces a self-satisfaction and dwells on itself while the task is neglected. No, His love was expressed in perpetual activity; even when He wept, was this not redeeming the time?[77]

This means that Jesus Christ, existentially judged, never failed to fulfill either the divine law or the specific will of his Father. He never made a gesture or conceived a plan which offended the most sensitive interpretation of the law of love.

> His life was pure love, and yet this whole life was only a single working day; He did not rest *until* the night came when He *could* no longer work; His labor did not cease with the changes of day and night, for when He was not working, then He watched in prayer. Thus was He the fulfillment of the law. And for a reward He demanded nothing, for His only requirement, His only purpose throughout His whole life from birth

---

[77] *Ibid.,* pp. 81-82.

to death, was to sacrifice Himself as an innocent victim — which not even the law in its most extreme demand — dared to demand. Thus was He the fulfillment of the law. The only one privy to His life, as it were, who was even able to follow Him, who was attentive enough and sleepless enough to follow Him, was the law itself, which followed Him step by step, hour by hour, with its infinite demand; but He was the fulfillment of the law.[78]

The inexhaustive potentialities of love as duty are brought to the attention when one remembers that the entire reach of law can be dissolved by a loving heart. New laws must continually be added to the existing body of law; but love, by taking in all conceivable law, renders the expedient of new law needless. It is true that law *limits* the exercise of selfishness, but love eliminates selfishness altogether.

Since God is love in his very essence, it is only when we conceive of God as the active agent in loving relations that we may pass from love on earth to heaven itself. Love is the true point of identity between time and eternity. This is why we are justified in saying that Kierkegaard's thesis, "Truth is subjectivity," is another way of describing the substance of love. The self is not existentially at its best apart from love, for God *is* love. "*Worldly wisdom* believes *that love is a relationship between man and man; Christianity teaches that love is a relationship between man — God — man, that is, that God is the middle term.*"[79] Christ is the absolute paradox for the very reason that he existentially mediated the duty of absolute love. The love which prevails on earth seldom rises to the heights manifested by Christ. Nor is this failure difficult to explain. Self-interest so thoroughly penetrates all human affection and understanding, that a condition of general depravity within mankind results.

Kierkegaard had a profound realization of the manner in which Christ lived by a divinely centered concept of love.

> He was, divinely understood, love. He loved by virtue of the divine understanding of what love is; He loved the entire race;

---

[78] *Ibid.*, pp. 82-83.
[79] *Ibid.*, p. 87.

He dared not — on account of His love, give up this, His understanding, for that would precisely be to deceive the race. Therefore His whole life was a terrible collision with the purely human understanding of what love is. It was the ungodly world which crucified Him; but even His disciples did not understand Him, and constantly sought to win Him to their conception of what love was, so that even to Peter He was obliged to say, "Get thee behind me, Satan." Unfathomable suffering in the terrible collision: that the most sincere, the most faithful disciple, when he, not only meaning well — oh, but burning with love — wishes to counsel Him for the best, wishes only to express how greatly he loves the Master — that this disciple, then, because he had a false conception of love, spoke in such a way that the Master must say to him: "You do not know it, but to me your words are as if it were Satan himself who spoke!" Thus Christianity came into the world, and with Christianity came the divine explanation of what love is.[80]

The pagan violence, which culminated in the crucifixion of Christ, remains a mystery unless we realize that those who carried out the act were guided by earthly rather than heavenly standards of righteousness. Partial love hates the one who takes up arms against partial love. And so, when Christ not only defended the duty of love for all, but lived by this standard, he suffered at the hands of those who presumed they were outstanding examples of love. "The love which does not lead to God, the love which does not have this as its sole goal, to lead the lovers to love God, stops at the purely human judgment as to what love and what love's sacrifice and submission are; it stops and thereby escapes the possibility of the last and most terrifying horror of the collision: that in the love relationship there are infinite differences in the idea of what love is."[81] Strife against Christ brought on the unique retaliation of the crucifixion because the pagan, who beheld righteousness incarnate, presumed that he could successfully do away with this judgment against his partiality.

Those who prefer partiality huddle together, basking in the resulting selfishness. "The world can never get any further in determining what love is, because it has neither God nor the

---
[80] *Ibid.*, p. 90.
[81] *Ibid.*, pp. 92-93.

neighbor as the middle term. What the world honors and loves under the name of love, is a union of selfishness."[82] Yet, the way of the world *is* a way of partial wisdom. One person performs a service for another, and the one receiving the benefits waits for a time to reciprocate. If all works well, mutual benefit results. But the difficulty is that the circle of fortune is easily broken. The arm of flesh will always fail.

Because love for God is the first and highest existential expression of the existing individual, the element of eternity makes it easier and more natural for one to love his neighbor. God does not seek love as an end in itself, as if he is hungry or empty. Quite to the contrary, God is absolute; he uses the Christian's love as a means by which he ensures love between those who see each other.

> Man must begin by loving the unseen, God, for thereby he will himself learn what it means to love; but the fact that he really loves the unseen will be recognized precisely by the fact that he loves the brother he sees; the more he loves the unseen, the more he will love the men he sees. Not conversely, that the more he rejects those he sees, the more he loves the unseen. If that were true then God would be transformed into an unreal something, a figment of the imagination. Therefore only a hypocrite and a deceiver would hit upon such ideas for the sake of finding an excuse; or one who misrepresents God by making it seem as if God were jealous for Himself and for being loved, instead of the blessed God being merciful, and, as it were, constantly subordinating Himself by saying: "If you will love me, then love the men you see; what you do to them you do to me."[83]

By approaching one's neighbor through the righteousness of God, *duty* is miraculously transformed into *debt*. In this way the seriousness of love to those on earth is increased. The result, in fact, is a duty/debt dialectic. The Christian is to owe a debt, but only one: love. This debt has a unique feature about it, for the more it is paid, the more it increases. The reason is that love is infinite. The more a person loves, the more he remains a debtor to love.

The height of existential ethics is reached when we realize

[82] *Ibid.*, pp. 97-98.
[83] *Ibid.*, p. 130.

that we are to *remain* in debt, forthrightly refusing all consolations that we have met the full terms of love. On the contrary, we should preserve an eternal vigilance in the heart, so that whether it be early or late, we shall determine to live by the plenitude of love, and never by partiality. "If you wish to preserve love, then you must preserve it in the infinite debt. Guard yourself, therefore, against comparisons!"[84] The true paradox of Christian ethics is evaded whenever the infinite duty of love is evaded. Evasion destroys the very being of the existing individual — spiritually and existentially understood — while surrender to duty brings suffering, for the duty of love connects the existing individual with eternity.

> Christianity says it is a duty to remain in debt, and means thereby that it *involves action, not a mere expression about love,* not a reflective *interpretation* of love. In the Christian sense no human being has ever accomplished the highest in love; and even if it were possible, this impossibility, there would at that very moment, from the Christian standpoint, be a new task. But if there is immediately a new task, then it is impossible to have time to know whether one has achieved the highest or not; for at the moment when one would get to know it, he is engaged in accomplishing the new task, and hence is prevented from knowing anything about the preceding moment, for which he has no time; he is occupied with the *haste of action,* whereas even in the moment of the greatest enthusiasm there is a certain lingering.[85]

None of this applies to the lover of this world, of course, since he is ignorant of God as the middle term in love. But when God is appreciated as the middle term, and when existence itself is suspended between an unavoidable duty and the equal impossibility of meeting it, then the possibility/impossibility dialectic has reached a place beyond which it cannot pass. Since the existential task is infinite, love, hope, and grace are our only sources of spiritual peace. There is no consolation whatever in the realization that the infinite has been partially met; for anything less than the infinite is finite, and everything finite falls short of the standards of righteousness imposed on

[84] *Ibid.,* p. 151.
[85] *Ibid.,* pp. 152-153.

the human race by God. All fulfillment traces to Jesus Christ, the God-man. "Even the most sincerely intended and, humanly speaking, the noblest enthusiasm, even the most fervent and disinterested enthusiasm, is still not earnestness, even though it accomplishes astonishing things, and even if it also wishes to remain in debt."[86]

Whenever a person turns from the infinite duty of love, he turns from Christianity itself. A Christian, if he is serious about his religious devotion, will tack passionately between infinite duty and the pain of temporal failure. In short, he will express repentance as well as love. Repentance is a mark of humility; it is nourished through faith and hope and the general experience of suffering.

This may disturb some individuals, but it will not disturb a dedicated Christian; for this *is* Christianity — at least, as Kierkegäard sought to develop it.

[86] *Ibid.*, p. 154.

Chapter Seven

YES AND NO

SINCE KIERKEGAARD BLENDED SOME VERY BRILLIANT INSIGHTS with some insights which (in our opinion at least) are not so brilliant, and since he did this in such a skillful yet frustrating manner, ideally a separate volume of critique should be written. But since the attainment of ideal goals must be left for others, we shall confine ourselves to a brief examination of what we believe are a few of the more prominent "yes" and "no" elements in Kierkegaard's general system.

A. *Yes*

First, when Kierkegaard looked at the church scene in his day, he did not particularly like what he saw. Not only were many professing Christians complacent about spiritual matters — thus forming what another has adroitly called "the cult of the uncommitted" — but an excessive affection for the things of this world was being expressed. Kierkegaard tried to make it clear, through the introduction of quite a variety of convincing arguments, that there is only *one* prudent way for a Christian to live, and that is by remembering at all times that God is God and man is man. Kierkegaard sought to clarify the meaning of total dependence upon God, in order that the existing individual might feel a sense of humility and thankfulness, even for the air he breathes. Unless we realize that we are dust, we are not likely to acknowledge that God is the creator of dust.

Kierkegaard correctly argued that only a fool would refuse to come to terms with his limitations. This particular type of foolishness, which traces to sin in the heart, fondly imagines that the self is sufficient unto itself. It thus goes along with the worldly notion that only weaklings confess that they are sinners. Presumably a robust individual can effectively manage by himself.

Even though the threat of physical death is always near at hand, a self-sufficient person either turns the other way, supposing, quite without proof, that physical death will in no way interrupt the continuity of life; or he somehow manages to persuade himself that this brief time on earth will fully satisfy his hunger for existence.

Kierkegaard very effectively replied that nothing less than the assurance of eternal happiness could appease the human breast. This truth should not only be acknowledged, but it should serve as a guide in life. A wise and consistent Christian will give an absolute devotion to an absolute *telos,* and a relative devotion to a relative *telos.* To reverse the elements in this teleology by giving absolute devotion to the relative and relative devotion to the absolute, is sin at its worst. In other words, this world deserves, and thus should receive, no more than relative passion; while the world above — and this includes *everything* which pertains to both the life and will of God — deserves, and thus should receive, absolute passion. Kierkegaard associated this balance of devotion with wisdom, and the Old Testament books of Proverbs and Ecclesiastes do the same. Moreover, Christ was perfect wisdom as well as perfect love, for he knew what was the right thing to do at the right time.

Second, Kierkegaard developed the meaning of Christian love with a profundity, thoroughness, and biblical accuracy which, it is no exaggeration to say, surpassed all previous efforts. Even though (to our knowledge) he never bothered to develop convincing rules of hermeneutics, he nonetheless had such a sense of biblical propriety that he was able to level a successful charge against the ethical standards of both the local Lutheran fellowship and the church at large. He was convinced — and rightly so — that far too many ethicists were quagmired in legalism. Consequently, the prevailing moral standards in Christianity seemed to be more relevant to the Old Testament than to the New.

Kierkegaard often gave the impression that the *real* man was the *ethical* man. But he did not reach his highest understanding of the relation between ethics and human nature until he recognized that love is the fulfillment of law, and that the ethical self falls short of its duties until it performs works of love.

This fusion of love and the nature of man is so realistic, and so in harmony with the specific teaching of Christ, that it is difficult to explain why so many professing Christian denominations, though asserting in their church ritual that love is the fulfillment of law, continue to place the highest emphasis upon the Ten Commandments. This is an indication of either prejudice or ignorance; for examine any form of wickedness — *any whatever* — and it will be discovered that the cause is a want of love.

When the precise terms of Christian love are understood, all ground for personal boasting is removed; for the existing individual *never* meets the full duties of the law of love. Christ alone met these duties.

And so it turns out that the more we learn about the meaning of love, the more we learn about the relation between God and this world. There are at least two reasons for this. One, God is love in his eternal essence. Two, when we existentially realize that we fall short of the duties of love, we are able to reject self-sufficiency so radically that it becomes natural to rest in God, morning, noon, and night, every day of the week. Since the duties of love are directly connected with eternity, divine grace is relevant to all stages on life's way.

Third, Kierkegaard then took the law of love and placed an *existential* interpretation on it. In doing this, he was not striving for social or academic status, for he realized that everything he said about the existing individual applied to *himself,* and that was painful at times.

To begin with, he decided that love and true existence are the same thing, for love is the law of life. It is not enough to *say* that we should love God with all our heart, and with all our soul, and with all our strength, and our neighbor as ourself. Unless we translate this testimony into active works of love, we do nothing which is particularly Christian.

Kierkegaard felt that the church of his day was doing little to help clarify the relation between Christian testimony and Christian living. This was a distressing neglect, for it meant that the existing individual, in the midst of a daily routine filled with fuss and flurry, was given little counsel about how to live. The average Christian had the mistaken notion that *assent* to orthodox doctrine was all that was required of him. Little wonder that Kierkegaard saw no essential difference between devils and professing Christians. By "professing Christians" he meant complacent individuals who recited the creeds of the church, but who made little or no spiritual (loving) effort to bring their lives into conformity with what they recited.

After Kierkegaard had carefully developed his criterion of existentialism, he made the climactic inference that an existing individual is *not* an existing individual unless he engages in works of love. This inference seems to create a contradiction, but let us remember that Kierkegaard was judging the ontology of the existing individual by *existential* and not by empirical or scientific criteria. Unless a Christian lives a life of love when he drives his automobile or when he walks through the market, he does nothing more than occupy space.

It may seem trite even to mention it, but as Christians we are to follow the example of Christ. This means that if we live as we should, we will develop a habit of love which not only issues in deeds of kindness toward others, but which draws us into the very presence of God. Whenever we are seriously engaged in works of love, we go far in setting forth public evidence that we are made in the image of God.

The term "existential" may strike some as nothing but a sign of academic pomposity, but it actually signifies that the *spiritual being* of a person has no reality apart from works of love. This should not be too difficult to accept.

B. *No*

First, Kierkegaard was content with a very inadequate relation between the Christian religion and public evidences. For example, he defended the possibility that a person is subjectively in the truth, even if he should happen to be related to what is not true. From this it would seem to follow that *any* religious position could be defended, providing a person held the position with sufficient subjective passion. Again, Kierkegaard said that a passionate idolater deserves more praise than a person who prays to the true God in a false spirit. Presumably the false spirit is that of complacency. Certainly complacency *is* a serious problem within the church, but it is difficult to see how the problem is in any way solved by canonizing passionate idolaters.

When Kierkegaard spoke of the Christian religion at another place, he made reference to the "unknown." This is a most interesting reference, for if something was unknown, how did Kierkegaard know enough to know that it was unknown? Moreover, how could *one* unknown be distinguished from *others*?

Although Kierkegaard said many fine things about faith, he was rather disappointing when he attempted to define the relation between faith and public evidences. He was so terrified by the prospect of complacency that he ended up asserting that faith is based on risk. He even went so far as to contend that the greater the risk, the greater the faith.

This was an unfortunate position to take, for with a little use of the imagination we can easily think of a paradox which is more offensive than the so-called absolute paradox, the incarnation. As long as there is no decisive relation between faith and public evidences, the imagination can devise new risks indefinitely. For example, what is to prevent us from asserting that Christ had two heads and spoke Chinese fluently — all in addition to what Kierkegaard had in mind when he referred to the absolute paradox? This hypothesis ought to increase our faith because it increases the risk we must take when we believe. But the fallacy in such a position is obvious — and it should have been obvious to Kierkegaard, too.

Now that we are concentrating our attention upon the relation between faith and public evidences, one further matter must be discussed. Kierkegaard said that certainty and passion do not go together. This is not a very convincing philosophic position to take, for certainty comes into being whenever the evidences are deemed sufficient. It makes no difference whether we are talking about *demonstration*, with which mathematics and formal logic deal, or about *probability*, with which all other branches of knowledge and science deal. As far as the state of certainty is concerned, *the one and only issue is the sufficiency of the evidences*. All else is beside the point. This means that apart from a state of certainty, we have no right to claim that we are in possession of truth. A Christian *may* respond to public evidences with passion, but passion has no more authority to create evidences for the Christian religion than it has to create evidences for the science of obstetrics. When all is said and done, therefore, passion and certainty are friends, not foes.

Some critics may reply that the epistemology to which we are appealing in our evaluation of Kierkegaard, falls apart because the meaning of "sufficiency" cannot be established. Such a criticism is without foundation, for sufficiency is simply a characteristic of evidences on which we are willing to act. For example, suppose I am walking down the sidewalk. I am certain that the sidewalk is safe because I am satisfied with the sufficiency of the evidences. In short, my act of walking is existential proof that I am experiencing a state of certainty. Whether or not I am passionate has nothing to do with the issue.

Kierkegaard seemed to have missed this elementary philosophic insight, and as a result he made some judgments about faith which are dreadfully weak. Unless the Christian religion is responsibly related to evidences which are both public and sufficient, it is simply not worth talking about.

Second, if we read Kierkegaard correctly, he failed to do justice to the doctrine of Christ's imputed righteousness. A great deal was said about the incarnation, and a little was said about the atonement; but one would need the lamp of Diogenes to find a systematic treatment of Christ's imputed righteousness. Since Kierkegaard labored so hard to establish the sinfulness of man, it is strange that he did not devote more attention to the specific question of how a sinner can find peace before a righteous God.

Classical theologians developed the concept of the filial bond in an effort to define the position into which a repentant sinner enters. But they also went on to make it clear that the only conceivable way in which a sinner could become an adopted son of God — at least the only way developed by the writers of Scripture — is through the imputed righteousness of Christ. Christ fulfilled both active and passive righteousness by his sinless life and by the offering up of his life upon the cross. All who establish the sincerity of their repentance by believing in Christ and by turning from their evil ways, are clothed about with the righteousness of Christ and are looked upon by God as adopted sons. Kierkegaard was simply magnificent in his defense of Christ's *active* righteousness (love), but he did not show the same zeal in the development of his soteriology. Two separate reasons may be suggested to help account for this.

First, students of Kierkegaard rather generally agree that he projected his view of God with a fear of his father before him. For example, in his address, "The Unchangeableness of God," Kierkegaard seemed to imply that there is terror in the very thought that God is unchangeable. The address as a whole is brilliant, to be sure, but this does not justify Kierkegaard's omission of the comforting truth that God is *love* in his very essence. Second, Kierkegaard may have entertained an unconscious fear that any emphasis upon Christ's imputed righteousness would have encouraged the existing individual to give up works of love and rest in an objectively apprehended soteriology. If Kierkegaard was so dedicated to the existential necessity of good works that salvation by faith alone was impossible, then at this point in his thinking he was closer to Roman Catholicism than he was to Protestantism.

Third, although a number of *minor* disappointments in Kierkegaard could be dealt with, we shall confine ourselves to one.

Kierkegaard had just about as unrealistic a grasp of the difference between male and female as one could have. He suggested that if a male by chance lusted after a young female, the female would experience dread (anxiety) as her first reaction, and then perchance she would experience indignation. But if a female lusted after a young male, the male would first of all experience abhorrence mingled with shame — and then dread. The reason for this difference, according to Kierkegaard, is that the male is more characterized by spirit than the female is.

It is difficult to conceive of any hypothesis which is further from the actual conditions which prevail in life. Yet, because Kierkegaard tried very hard to cultivate valid grounds for a sense of humor in Christians, perhaps here would be a place to have a good laugh. Certainly Kierkegaard's view of the difference between male and female is so void of truth that it is funny.

We can be glad that Kierkegaard was not this far from reality when he developed the main points in his system. If he had consistently misread the true state of things, his books could be thrown into the nearest junk pile. But because he didn't do this, but rather strove to enrich the body of Christ by developing a fresh interpretation of spiritual truth, his books should be read, and read again.

Let us close with this brief summary: *Kierkegaard was a genius in his ability to bring man closer to God, and God closer to man. His guiding rule was that an absolute devotion should be given to an absolute* telos, *and a relative devotion to a relative* telos. *With the help of this rule, Kierkegaard succeeded in defining an existential approach to the existing individual. This approach is exciting, to say the least.*

INDEX

Abraham, 126-132
Anfechtung, 130-1
Aristotle, 13, 64, 124

Christianity (Christian), 34ff., 62-3, 71-2, 81, 83, 85, 87, 90, 98-9, 101, 106-7, 110-13, 115-17, 122, 132-3, 138-140, 144-5, 158, 161, 164, 168, 170
Copenhagen, 36, 62, 72, 122

Despair, 81, 112, 121, 125, 133, 146, 151-2, 156
Dialectic, 46, 54, 56, 75, 81, 90, 98, 105-6, 108-10, 133, 136, 155-6, 162-3
Doctrine, 36, 122-3, 144
Dread (anxiety), 17, 20-22, 41, 47-8, 74ff., 112, 117, 129, 133, 151, 171-2

Eternity, 47, 50-1, 53-5, 60, 65, 67-8, 71, 77-8, 81-3, 85-6, 99, 105-6, 110-11, 134, 139-40, 144-6, 148-52, 154, 157-60, 163, 166-7
Ethics (ethical), 49-50, 53, 59, 67ff., 72, 78, 85, 93, 95-7, 105-6, 108-9, 111-2, 127-31, 136, 142, 145, 147, 149-50, 153ff., 162-3, 167
Existential, 33, 35, 37, 41, 44n., 45, 48-9, 53, 57, 60-1, 66-7, 70, 74, 77, 79, 81, 84, 86, 88, 92, 101, 103-4, 106, 108-9, 111, 114-5, 118-9, 121, 132, 135-7, 139-40, 142, 146, 148-9, 153, 156, 159-60, 162, 167-8, 170-2

Faith, 41, 70-1, 84, 86-8, 92, 97-8, 112-7, 120-2, 124-34, 136, 143, 152, 164, 169, 171
Freedom (spirit), 26-7, 44-9, 54-5, 66, 69, 74-6, 78, 110, 122, 142, 151-2, 156

God, 33-5, 39, 42, 50-2, 72-3, 88-9, 96-8, 101, 115-22, 124-6, 133-5, 137, 140-7, 151, 154-6, 160-1, 163-9, 171-2
Guilt, 59-60, 75ff., 97, 134-5, 144

Hegel, 21, 26, 90, 100ff.
Hope, 54, 66, 70, 79, 136, 147ff., 156, 163-4
Humor, 58-60, 99, 102, 142-4

Immanence, 51-2, 85-7, 126, 138, 148
Immediacy, 60-1, 133, 135-6
Incarnation, 52, 83, 85-6, 96, 111-3, 116-7, 119-20, 132-3, 160, 169-170
Individual, 26ff., 31-4, 46, 53, 95, 103-6, 108-11, 113, 125-6, 132, 134, 136, 141, 144-5, 147, 153, 156, 158-9, 162-3, 165, 167-8, 171-2
Instant, 50, 52-3, 55, 71

Love, 41, 54-5, 78, 110, 118-9, 153ff., 166-8

Mediation, 49, 82, 106, 110
Melancholy, 15-16, 41, 66, 79-80

Niebuhr, Reinhold, 47, 54, 87, 132

173

Objectivity, 33, 35, 38, 48-50, 72, 86-7, 99, 102, 110ff., 121-3, 125-6, 132-3, 135
Olsen, Regina, 21-24

Paradox, 34, 51-2, 73-5, 83-4, 86, 88, 96-8, 106, 109, 111-3, 116-7, 126-7, 132-4, 139, 141-2, 148, 160, 169
Pascal, 39-40
Philosophy (philosopher), 36, 38, 48-9, 61-2, 64, 72-3, 91ff., 100ff., 107-8, 114, 122, 138, 170

Poet, 63-4, 137-8

Repentance, 59, 142, 144, 159, 164, 171

Self-interest (self-love), 27, 155, 158, 160

Sin, 73, 77ff., 86-7, 98, 112, 125, 132, 134, 159, 166, 170-1

Socrates, 28-31, 38, 44-51, 57, 80, 82, 93, 100-1, 109-10, 121-2, 132

Subjectivity, 38, 49, 53, 56, 68, 72, 79, 86-87, 90-1, 97, 99-100, 102, 110-14, 116-19, 122, 124ff., 140, 153, 155, 158, 160, 169

Suffering, 72, 84, 134-147, 156, 163

www.ingramcontent.com/pod-product-compliance
Lightning Source LLC
Chambersburg PA
CBHW051932160426
43198CB00012B/2122